THE SWORD
OF THE SPIRIT

Audrey Augustine Mrofchak

PUBLISHING COMPANY
P.O. Box 42028 Santa Barbara, CA 93140-2028
(800) 647-9882 • (805) 957-4893 • Fax: (805) 957-1631

©1998 Queenship Publishing

Library of Congress Number: 97-65314

Published by:
       Queenship Publishing
       P.O. Box 42028
       Santa Barbara, CA 93140-2028
       (800) 647-9882 (805) 957-4893 Fax: (805) 957-1631

ISBN: 1-882972-95-3

Printed in the United States of America

PREFACE

This book was written in obedience to two theologians and several priests who counseled me throughout the years.

Secondly, it was written in obedience to a word of prophecy which was given, "Write a book about your knowledge of Me. In the latter days it will be a testimony to Me."

Thirdly, it was written in obedience to my family and Christian friends who consistently said, "Write these things down."

Contents

–1–

Harden Not Your Hearts

I had been taught that "obedience is better than sacrifice" (*1 Sam.* 15:22 TJB); and in that spirit of obedience to God's Word, and that of several spiritual directors who helped to guide me in the way of God's Spirit, I now undertake to recount in writing my spiritual walk with the Lord. But in order for the reader to comprehend this true story, he must go back with me to the time when it all began and see how it gradually evolved to the present time.

I was born in the 1930's during the struggle of the Depression years, when my family realized what hardships were. Mother passed away at the young age of twenty-two, when my brother and I were just toddlers. The tragic loss of my mother left me with a deep heartache and a feeling of emptiness. Instinctively, I turned to God and found that He was a loving Father. In my insecurity, I clung to Him in total dependency, fearful less the tide of life engulf me. Although He had not yet revealed Himself, I felt the comfort of the Spirit's abiding love. I would pour out my heart to Him in a childish way, without realizing that this was true prayer.

It was during those formative years of childish murmurings, of childhood prayers, that God's Spirit responded to me by speaking a word in the depth of my heart. Such a spiritual word is known as the *rayma*. In time, those loving talks became spiritual walks and wanderings; I would follow wherever His Spirit would lead. He occasionally would give me a foretaste of things to come. For me, events would occur in the spiritual realm years before they took place in our temporal world. I began to experience these prophetic insights at the tender age of five or six. Because I was so young, naturally I did not comprehend what this all meant. I knew only that the Father was doing a work, and I simply watched.

One day, when I was in my seventh year and was attending church, something very unusual happened. After I had received Holy Communion and was adoring the Lord, my spirit was caught up to an unknown place. From a great height I was shown the Heavenly Jerusalem. This fantastic sight was beyond anything we can imagine. Later on, I learned that such an experience is called ecstatic prayer, in which one's spirit is caught up in a rapture, or a flight of the spirit.

This ecstatic prayer can only take place by the will of God, who intends some great work or understanding to come from it. Now I have come to realize that God had spoken a prophetic word about the Messianic Jerusalem in that vision. The Lord did not permit me to grasp the entire meaning of this revelation at so young an age, for it was not the proper season to taste the unripened fruit of this experience. I had to wait for the right season in time. I did not speak to anyone about this, for I could not comprehend it myself; but I have never forgotten that day or that vision, although it took place almost forty years ago.

Years later I learned that such an initial experience could be a call from the Lord to a contemplative or mystic vocation. We have the teaching of Abbot D. Lehodey to rely on in this regard:

> If a soul has already received a beginning of mystical union, it has always been admitted that she may desire further progress in these ways. God had given a true vocation and deposited a germ; to desire that this should be developed is to will what God wills.[1]

Perhaps this will be difficult for some to believe, but the following quotation from learned scholars gives evidence that these events are possible, and have taken place in the lives of very young children. For example,

The age at which the saints became ecstatics. Dr. Imbert has compiled the following table: St. Hildegard, Catherine of Siena, at the age of 4; St. Peter of Alcantara, Blessed Osanna of Manua, St. Angela of Brescia, Mother Agnes of Jesus (of Langeac), at 6 years of age; Blaise of Caltanisetta, at 7; Christina of Stommeln, at 11; St. Agnes of Montepulciano, at 14; Mary of Agreda, at 18; Veronica of Binasco, at 40; and St. Teresa, at 43. (Vol. II, ch. xvii, p. 276).[2]

So, you see that deep spiritual experiences and prayers are possible for children, even ecstatic prayer. I personally know of two children who have related this type of prayer to me, but they were unaware of how significant their experiences were. It is a tragic loss to the Christian Community to push such children aside simply because they are young. Adults thereby arrest the spiritual development of these little ones who they believe have only "flights of fancy." Let us pray for greater discernment in listening to the children's spiritual experiences and welcome them as Christ has requested us to do. "Whoever welcomes this little child on my account welcomes me..." (*Lk.* 9:48 NAB).

Because I had no one with whom to share my spirituality, I had no direction and drifted along in the routine life of adolescence and young adulthood. Years later, the Lord drew me back to Himself into the profound relationship we once had by speaking another word to me. But we shall take this up later. Let us first try to understand the different ways that the Lord speaks to men.

Many times when He desires to communicate His words to us, we find that we are not prepared to receive that precious blessing, due either to our ignorance or to our hard-heartedness, which makes us turn a deaf ear to Him. Let us search the Scriptures to see what the Spirit has to teach about God's communication to man. "Today, if you should hear his voice, harden not your hearts as at the revolt in the day of testing in the desert." (*Heb.* 3:7, 8 NAB).

We notice here that although the Lord spoke to our ancestors, they steeled their hearts against His word and sinned; they were unable to grasp His ways. "The word which they heard did not profit them, for they did not receive it in faith." (*Heb.* 4:3 NAB). Regardless of how often the Lord spoke through His prophets, the people would not listen. "Then, the Lord of hosts in his great anger said that as they had not listened when he called, so he would not listen when they called." (*Zech.* 7:13 NAB). And the people were scattered; and only a faithful remnant, known as the Anawim, remained. Their expectant faith and attentiveness to His word enabled them to receive God's blessings, for they realized that "not by bread alone does man live, but by every word that comes forth from the mouth of the Lord." (*Dt.* 8:3 NAB). Because the well-springs of life hinge upon man's response to God, we can begin to fathom the importance of His word, no matter how it is communicated to us.

The Lord speaks to us through world events, the Church, through Scriptures, and sometimes through spiritual manifestations such as prophetic words, visions, and supernatural dreams. For example, in a dream God spoke to Joseph and instructed him to take Mary and Jesus to Egypt because Herod planned to kill the Child. Likewise, St. John the Evangelist heard the word of the Lord through the vehicle of prophetic vision, and wrote about that word in the *Apocalypse.* So too, God spoke to Moses from the burning bush and commissioned him to deliver His people from slavery.

These men searched for the reality of God in prayer, and the Lord revealed Himself to them by means of supernatural word. Their prayerful dialogue united them in a close relationship with God. The inspired *Psalms* of David were the perfect expression of this spiritual relationship. Many people living in Christian communities today are being inspired by the Holy Spirit to write songs of worship and praise which are similar to the *Psalms*. In some instances we can hear the word of the Lord contained within these songs of worship, but only those who have a keen sense of discernment are able to hear it.

The mode of communication that God chooses to use is not so important. What is absolutely necessary is that we receive His life-giving word with expectant hearts. We must be attentive to what the Lord is saying today lest He leave us as impoverished as the Israelites who sinned against Him in the desert.

Like the majority of people, it never entered my mind that God would have something to say to me—and because of this notion I nearly missed His message, or word, to me. Twenty years ago, I again heard His word spoken in my heart, this time in the form of a locution. Now, a locution is a mode of expression whereby we hear or understand words of supernatural origin as they convey God's will.

It happened like this: One quiet night, He said, "Why don't you make a retreat?" These words startled me — yet, because of their effect, I knew they had been spoken by the Lord. The following day I inquired and learned that there was a retreat house nearby. I phoned and was informed that one vacancy was left for the next scheduled retreat. Three days later, without a notion of what to expect, I arrived to begin my retreat. This was to be a silent retreat. We were told to meditate upon God and reflect upon our relationship with Him. How little did I realize the surprises the Holy Spirit had in store for me!

Since I had no teaching on the structures of meditation, I simply talked and walked informally with the Lord, as I had previously done as a child. With the grace of God I was able to close out the distractions of the world. Focusing my thoughts upon the Lord, I imagined that He and I were alone and walking upon the face of the earth together as we discussed many things.

At that time I discovered a new awareness of the Presence of God and found that He is not as inaccessible as I had thought. For a short while things were quite pleasant; then, the Lord began to deal with me in His own way. He showed me areas of my life which were not to His liking. The Spirit enlightened my consciousness and brought to the surface all my wrongdoings since I had reached the age of reason. I had lived as most Catholics do, had gone to church and had received the Sacraments, but for some reason the Lord wanted a deeper purification of my soul. Things took on a serious note.

As the hours passed by, the prayerful silence deepened and the grace of a profound repentance began to well up inside of me. In a general way I repented of all the wrongdoing in my life. It brought to mind what St. Peter had said on Pentecost: "You must reform and be baptized ... then you will receive the gift of the Holy Spirit. It was to you and your children that the promise was made, and to all those still far off whom the Lord calls." (*Acts* 2:38-40 NAB).

The Lord had called me there. Was I one of those far off children? Surely, He had called me there for a purpose.

This heart-rending repentance unlocked the door to a tremendous encounter with the Lord. What great joy poured into my heart! I felt a magnificent kind of freedom and realized that "...if the son frees you, you will be free." (*Jn.* 8:36 NAB). I perceived my Lord through the blessings He had brought with Him — the fruit of His Spirit, peace, love, and joy. My long loneliness vanished as I clung to this Father once again.

The Bible states that the only way to break through the barrier between us and the Lord is through the avenue of repentance. Millions seek to know Him and strain their ears to hear His word, but when He speaks they do not recognize His voice. Thus, they fail in their endeavor to find Him.

One of the reasons for this tragic failure is the fact that most people seek Him only half-heartedly, and that lukewarm desire is not sufficient to open the floodgates of His powerful grace. "When you look for me, you will find me. Yes, when you seek me with ALL your heart." (*Jer.* 29:13 NAB). It was only through hard experience that I learned this myself. In order to receive ALL, I had to surrender ALL with a loving heart. You see, there are no half measures in His kingdom. But realize this, that what you surrender is so pitifully small, in comparison to that which you receive, that your so-called sacrifice is not even worth mentioning.

How insignificant His invitation to the retreat seemed to be; yet, because it was from the Lord, it carried with it all the conviction needed to move me into the direction that He desired. Although the Spirit invites us, He leaves us the freedom to decide whether to accept His blessings or not. The decision is surely ours. God's greatest desire is to give us His abundant life, but through ignorance we often deny Him that opportunity.

When I responded whole-heartedly to His call or invitation, the Lord moved my entire being into the sphere of His redemptive activity. Grace alone enabled me to surrender to that word, and His word did not return to Him void, but effected a fantastic change within me. He lovingly accepted my repentance, and my fountain of tears was transformed into a fountain of living water, which is symbolic of the Holy Spirit. My spirit was filled to overflowing, and I wanted to leap and sing in the Presence of the Lord, who said, "Whoever drinks the water I shall give him will never thirst; no, the water I give shall become a fountain within him leaping up to provide eternal life." (*Jn.* 4:14 NAB).

Now you see, Jesus offers this living water to everyone, but not everyone receives it and drinks it. Drinking from this fountain of living water brought forth in me a new life which was filled with His Spirit. Under the inspiration and breath of the Holy Spirit, a new creativity developed within me and gave my life a strange, new spiritual dimension. The release of the Spirit within me was just the beginning of what abundant life is all about.

My whole life took on new meaning. I became excited as I saw the unceasing activity of God all around. I became hungry to know God more perfectly and to possess Him as much as possible in this world. A great zeal for the work of the Lord filled my being as this baptism of fire began to burn. This continual short prayer came to mind repeatedly: "O Holy Spirit, consume me until I become a torch of fire for Thee."

I began to make annual retreats, for the recollection of tremendous encounter with the Lord was all the incentive I needed to return to that house of prayer. The peaceful atmosphere helped me to be attentive to His word, and the song of silence became lovable.

It was at this retreat place that I heard the Lord speak again in a different way. While I was contemplating the Passion of Christ, my attention was drawn towards the tabernacle, where the Eucharist is reserved. I heard and saw, as if written in fire, coming toward me like lightning, these words: "I love you." There are no words sufficient to describe the unworthiness I felt at that moment. Even now when recalling this incident, I can only think of the great condescension and mercy of the Almighty toward so poor a creature. What explanation can be offered for such things?

Years later, I found reference to a similar experience in St. John of the Cross's book *The Living Flame of Love*, which explains that God does indeed speak to souls who have repented and have gone through certain purifications. He cited the words of Jeremiah: "Is not my word like fire, says the Lord, like a hammer shattering rocks?" (*Jer.* 23:29 NAB).

His words came unto me that day as fire and entered into my heart as if lightning had struck. I knew that thereafter I would never be the same. Not all God's words have this type of effect upon us, but there are certain words, comparable to a spiritual touch, which do this.

By degrees, I grew more sensitive to God's word, for my ears had been circumcised by the Holy Spirit. After Communion one day, the Lord spoke a different type of word within my heart, saying, "They have pierced My hands and My feet." This pitiful lament from the Eucharistic Lord had such an effect upon me that I could not refrain from weeping. It is one thing to recite the prayer containing these words, and quite another thing to hear them from the lips of Christ.

The measure with which our worship of the Eucharistic Lord is pure will determine the degree to which the Lord responds. So few believe in the sacramental presence of Christ, and this disbelief sadly hinders the Lord from fully manifesting Himself to His people. Surely we cannot expect to receive God's benediction if we do not render unto Him the esteem He so rightly deserves.

By these various experiences, the Lord was progressively teaching me how to comprehend His word. I began to see things in the light of God's viewpoint. Daily my confidence and love for Him increased. When the Lord sees someone relying on His word, He moves into the center of his belief and fulfills that which He has spoken. "I no longer speak of you as slaves, for a slave does not know what his master is about. Instead, I call you friends, since I have made known to you all that I heard from my Father." (*Jn.* 15.15 NAB).

Today more believers are hearing His word in simple prophecy, called prophetic utterances, and sometimes through the means of locutions. This is not unusual, for the Spirit communicated His word in like manner to the early Church. God also speaks to us through His prophets, and what I see happening in Christian communities is the fulfillment of the prophecy of Joel: "Then afterwards I will pour out my spirit upon all mankind. Your sons and daughters shall prophesy..." (*Joel* 3:1 NAB). My personal reception of His word is just one instance of what God is doing on a larger scale within the entire world.

This spiritual experience which I had can be explained as the opening of two sealed doors — the doors to my heart and to my understanding. By responding to Him, I found that He had permitted me to enter into the mysterious depths of His Paschal mystery. This is what life in Christ was all about.

Jesus calls everyone to enter into this sublime mystery, but only you can unlatch those sealed doors. "If one of you hears me calling and opens the door, I will come in to share his meal side by side with him." (*Rev.* 3:20 NAB). Imagine, the Lord of Lords wants to enter your heart to share a meal with you, now! He will not wait until the world passes away. How can this take place? You must first invite Him into your heart as the Lord of your whole life, and He will come in and sup with you in spiritual communion, which is a prelude to the bliss which awaits us in Heaven. In time He will increase your knowledge of Him by opening up the door of your understanding, also.

As you can see, then, Jesus is leading His people to something far greater than repentance, although this is the first step to take. He eagerly invites ALL to another supper, which will be magnificent; it will be His wedding feast with His Church. We are instructed to be prepared for the Master's return: "Let your belts be fastened around your waists and your lamps be burning ready. Be like men awaiting their master's return from a wedding, so that when he arrives and knocks, you will open for him without delay." (*Lk.* 12:36 NAB). "It will go well with those servants whom the master finds wide awake on his return." (*Lk.* 12:37 NAB).

As in the parable, Jesus is the Master who is with us to the end of the world. He has not left His children as orphans. He cautions us to be prepared for His Second Coming so that He can bring us to His celestial banquet. His Spirit invites you and prepares you for this glorious feast, as His word tells us: "I am indeed going to prepare a place for you, and then I shall come back to take you with me that where I am you also may be." (*Jn.* 14:3 NAB).

Jesus also cautions us to have our lamps lit. What lamp is He referring to? Now this lamp is the symbolic fire of the Holy Spirit, which should make us glow like lampstands aflame with the indwelling Presence of the Lord. When the Lord returns to take His people to the celestial nuptials, He expects them to be clothed in the wedding garment of sanctifying light, which His Holy Spirit weaves. Without His Spirit, there would be no fire, no light, and no garment; and, those without this garment will be unable to enter His nuptials.

"Stay awake, because you do not know the day when your Master is coming." (*Matt.* 24:42 TJB). Are we spiritually asleep when He speaks a word to awaken us to a new dimension of life? I tremble at the thought that I might not have listened to His word.

I hungered for the sweet knowledge of eternal life which is Christ. Like a starved person, I devoured His spiritual food. What privileged people we are, for the Lord, who is a loving Father, feeds His children the best of food. "Open up your mouth and I will fill it." (*Ps.* 81:11 NAB). The Lord has supplied us with this spiritual food in order to transform us into supernatural people who in turn will produce spiritual fruit. The fruit which we can offer to Him is the spiritual sacrifice of praise, which is the fruit of our lips. (*Heb.* 13:15 TJB). The Father looks for His children who are willing to worship Him in the truth and in the Spirit. In *Genesis*, we see that Abel offered the Lord the first fruits of the land, and God was pleased. So too must we offer God the first fruit of our spirit: praise—so that we also may be pleasing to the Lord.

So now we see that Jesus has called a people who will share in His fruitful action through the power of His Spirit. And when the precious fruit of His Spirit has matured and ripened, He will send forth His servants to bring in the harvest which He has planted through His death and resurrection. Praise God!

–2–

Contemplating God's Mysteries

As I walked deeper into the obscurity of this spiritual desert, I was given a new song, and the prayer of David was upon my lips: "Yahweh, teach me your ways, how to walk beside you faithfully." (*Ps.* 86:11 TJB). Once more I asked Him which direction I should take, for I knew that He saw me wandering and knew of my thirst. His Spirit directed me with these words: "Inquire about the ancient paths; which was the good way? Take it then, and you shall find rest." (*Jer.* 6:16 TJB). When I pondered upon these words, He quickly brought me to a place of rest, where His Spirit taught me. He generously quenched my thirst by offering me more of His "living water," which I sipped from the golden cup of contemplation. He gave me this Scripture: "And I am going to show you a way that is better than any of them." (*1 Cor.* 13:31 TJB).

This "ancient pathway," or the "better way," was the way of love. All other ways would fail, but love alone would never end. (*1 Cor.* 13:8 TJB). Thus the merciful God took pity upon my poverty and set my spirit upon the pathway of affective love, where I would find a greater awareness of His presence—both interiorly and exteriorly.

Only the Spirit of God can initiate contemplative prayer by conferring the grace to focus the spiritual powers within our nature upon Himself in a loving, intensive gaze. Contemplation deepens the interpersonal relationship with God, thereby greatly effecting a deep spiritual transformation. As this transformation evolves, the spiritual insight broadens, both intuitively and intellectually, as a result of the direction of God's Spirit. The effects of this prayer of union between God and man is an infusion of God-given knowledge which manifests itself not through intellectual achievement, but through a total embrace of the Word in love.

It is impossible in the scope of this book to summarize the various degrees of contemplative prayer which are open to Christians. Those who are seeking such knowledge would benefit by reading St. Teresa of Avila's works and *The Ascent of Mount Carmel* by St. John of the Cross. There are also many excellent examples of contemplative prayer in Scripture. Right now, let us be content to define only two major types of the prayer of contemplation.

These two categories of contemplative prayer are "acquired" contemplation and "infused," or mystical, contemplation. In acquired contemplation, a person, aided by the grace of God, prepares his heart and mind to receive some supernatural truth pertaining to the life of Christ or an insight into the mystery of faith.

On the other hand, in the case of infused or mystical contemplation, a person is consciously aware of the powerful indwelling presence of God, who suspends the natural activity of the person so that he may be silently attentive to the operations of God's Spirit in whatever manner he chooses. That person should be intent upon discovering the full meaning and implications of God's movements. The laity as well as the religious can enjoy contemplative prayer, which is the result of a very intimate relationship with the Lord.

I myself am a lay woman who has experienced this type of contemplation while moving through the routine of everyday life. I also have found that many biblical figures, employed in the midst of the world, were granted this prayer of contemplation. One of the best examples of New Testament contemplative prayer is the story of Martha and Mary.

On a journey, Jesus entered a village where a woman named Martha welcomed Him to her home. She had a sister named Mary, who seated herself at the Lord's feet and listened to His tales of hospitality. Martha came to Him and said, "Lord, are you not concerned that my sister has left me to do the household tasks all alone? Tell her to help me." The Lord in reply said to her: "Martha, Martha, you are anxious and upset about many things; one thing only is required. Mary has chosen the better portion, and she shall not be deprived of it." (*Lk.* 10:38-41 NAB).

In this story we observe a close friendship between Jesus and the two sisters of Lazarus. He was welcomed in their home and in their hearts. They realized that He was very special. Yet, unlike many people in our day, these sisters adored Him without reciting long formal prayers. They simply conversed with Him and visited in an informal way. Preoccupied Martha was a believer, but she was not fully attentive to the Presence of God in Christ. Meditative Mary, on the other hand, seemed to grasp immediately the significance of this Presence, sat lovingly at the Master's feet and focused her mind and heart entirely upon Him. He wanted their undivided attention so that they could receive the wisdom that He would impart. The receptive Mary had chosen "the better part," and the Lord began to reveal to her "the ancient pathway of His love." Her positive response of self enabled her to receive the outpouring gift of contemplation.

She was at the Master's feet in that state of rest, where she ceased her own activity in order to receive God's active word, which had the power to renew and recreate her. The creation of the world was brought forth by the word of God. "He said, 'Let there be light,' and there was light." (*Gen.* 1:3 TJB). When Jesus spoke His word to Mary, His life-giving word became activated Light within her, re-creating her into a new creature; for He was "the real light which gives light to every man." (*Jn.* 1:9 NAB). Because she had grasped His ways, she was now able to enter "a place of rest reserved for God's people." (*Heb.* 4:9, 10 TJB). She had found that which all Israel could not find because they were not attentive to His word.

Do you see the tremendous wisdom contained in this Scripture? Mary had entered into the initial stages of contemplative prayer because Jesus had found a creature who was willing to receive the outpouring of His heart in a "word gift." Scripture teaches, "Now I will pour out my heart to you, and tell you what I have to say." (*Prov.* 1:23 TJB). "For the Lord gives wisdom, from his mouth come knowledge and understanding." (*Prov.* 2:6 NAB).

Jesus is still seeking for those "special people" to whom He can pour out His heart. He is seeking those who will receive His testimony of heavenly mysteries. "The one who comes from heaven testifies to what he has seen and heard, but no one accepts his testimony... The one whom God has sent speaks the words of God; he does not ration his gift of the Spirit." (*John* 3:31-34 NAB).

By observing the humble, receptive attitude of Mary, we can learn how to profit by listening to the word which God speaks in our hearts. "Trust in the Lord with all your heart, on your own intelligence rely not; in all your ways be mindful of him, and he will make straight your paths." (*Prov.* 3:5, 6 NAB).

This path that He wants to make straight is the "ancient path" of love. He expects His people to abound in charity, for love fulfills the law. By opening up the door to your heart, you can also receive His "word gift," His Light, His friendship, and His abiding Presence. He will draw you into a deep relationship with the Father through the Spirit. He will teach you then, even as He did Mary.

Some books present contemplation in such a difficult way that few Christians are encouraged to aspire to it. Yet, many people can attain it because they receive this prayer by the way of LOVE, and all people, great and small, are capable of loving. "God is love and anyone who lives in love lives in God and God lives in him." (*1 John* 4:16 TJB). These lovers of God will receive the knowledge of His wisdom through the union of their hearts with the will of God.

Although one can prepare himself for this contemplative union with God by living a mature Christian life and all that it implies, this is not a state of prayer which one can grasp at will. Growing in spiritual maturity requires time, but the Lord's eyes are upon the just, and He watches those who seek Him with a heart-rending desire. When a person opens himself daily to the graces of God, he will begin to see God move in a dynamic way within his life. In the meantime, one must practice great detachment from all that would hinder this union, together with patience and perseverance in prayer. "Good is the Lord to one who waits for him, to the soul that seeks him." (*Lam.* 3:25 NAB).

Let us now examine a deeper level of contemplation shown in Scripture—the prayer of Abraham, the man of faith.

Abraham, the great patriarch, encountered the God he worshipped many times. When he first experienced the Lord directly, he heard this word: "Leave your country." (*Gen.* 12:1 TJB). His faithful response to that word, together with a supreme detachment from everything he had known, compelled him to journey into an unknown land. Yahweh blessed his obedience by drawing Abraham into a profound relationship with Himself. We can see this union of wills in the frequency that dialogues between Abraham and the Lord took place. Often the Lord would reveal His Presence to Abraham by means of visions. The high peak of Abraham's spiritual life took place when God ratified the Covenant with him and all his descendants. During this time Abraham fell into what seemed like a deep sleep, but it was in reality ecstatic prayer. His physical senses were suspended while a great darkness enveloped him.

In the writings of the Saints and mystics we often find mention of God's manifesting His Presence in this ray of blinding contemplation. Because of mankind's weak nature he is unable to bear such glory, and his humanity is abashed at the revelation. St. Paul experienced this ray of blinding contemplation on the road to Damascus.

Now, as this ecstatic vision with Abraham unfolded, "there appeared a smoking furnace and a firebrand." (*Gen.* 15:17,18 TJB). When the Covenant was sealed, a filial relationship was established between the Lord and Abraham. This Covenant relationship was extended to all those who belonged to the lineage of Abraham, even to the present day. We see this pattern of the Spirit's action repeated through history as He refashions His creation into a new form. St. James described this when he wrote, "He wills to bring us to birth with a word spoken in truth, so that we may be a kind of first fruits of his creatures." (*James* 1:18 NAB).

Throughout the ages we notice this identical experience unfolding within the lives of such Covenant people as Joseph, Daniel, Moses and the prophets, and on into the New Testament with the disciples and those He called His friends. "I call you friends, because I have made known to you everything I learnt from my Father." (*John* 15 TJB). The Lord teaches the mysteries of His kingdom to those who have this type of relationship with Him. He not only teaches them, but He brings them into that place of God's rest by means of contemplative prayer.

King David petitioned the Lord in prayer to give him this rest, for he sang, "Rest in God alone, my soul!" (*Ps.* 62:5 TJB). Day and night he called upon the name of Yahweh and patiently waited upon the visitation of the Lord. He had never heard of the beatitude of the pure of heart, but the Spirit prompted him to seek purity, for he wrote, "Make me single-hearted in fearing your name." (*Ps.* 86:11 TJB). He knew intuitively that he could not see God unless his heart were pure. He intensely desired to see the Lord, yet he feared even His name. It was, however, this same reverential fear which opened up the gateway to infused contemplation which we see throughout the book of *Psalms*. By persistent prayer, King David received the Word into his heart. He experienced the indwelling of God's Spirit. We have evidence of this, as David frequently prophesied His word.

Jesus had often proclaimed that purity of heart was a necessary condition for one to "see" God. "Blessed are the single hearted for they shall see God." (*Matt.* 5:8 NAB). Since this is the one condition which is necessary for so great a grace, it behooves us to make every effort to cleanse our hearts of sin. Each part of the interior being must be purified, sanctified, and totally consecrated to Him in order to grow in the knowledge of His indwelling Presence. But the purification which is so necessary cannot take place until we have opened up our hearts in order to receive that transforming power of God's Spirit which is able to recreate us into new creatures in Christ. "Circumcise your heart then and be obstinate no longer." (*Deut.* 10:16 TJB).

If we do not heed His words, then we can have no part with Him. We will not be able to enter into His Body, which He referred to as a temple. "No alien, uncircumcised in heart and body, is to enter my sanctuary." (*Ezek.* 44:9 TJB). The Lord is not speaking about a temple made by hands, but of the Temple of His Body of believers. We have no right to enter into His spiritual Body until we have received this covenant relationship signified by the circumcision of the heart. Jesus demands that every unclean thing within our hearts be "cast out." In response to our repentance, the Lord in turn will mercifully change our inner being, as He said, "I will give you a new heart, and place a new spirit within you taking from your bodies your stony hearts and giving you natural hearts. I will put my spirit within you and make you live by my statutes, careful to observe my decrees." (*Ezek.* 36:26, 27 NAB). As He purifies our beings, He anoints us with His Spirit, for "the real circumcision is in the heart, something not of the letter but of the spirit." (*Rom.* 2:29 TJB). When this happens we become aware that a wonderful transformation is taking place deep within us, changing us into new creatures.

Twenty years ago, as I was reading from Peter De Caussade's book *Abandonment to Divine Providence,* these words stood out from the page: "Ask Me for a pure heart." This prompting of His Spirit had such a tremendous effect upon me that I began to pray daily for this blessing. I sensed a new spiritual activity within as time passed by, but I could not define it.

I was intently seeking the Lord and awaiting a response hopefully. What father can watch his child reach out to him with arms of faith and love without being affected? The Lord touches such a one and gives him a greater knowledge of Himself. Many times while I contemplated the Lord's life in this way, utterances would begin to flow from my heart which expressed the sentiments I was then feeling. In this fashion, a loving dialogue began to develop between the Lord and myself. He gave me songs and prayers, which were uttered through the Spirit, who is often called the lyric singer of the soul. I began to write some of these responses down and was surprised to see the great similarity between them and the *Psalms* of David.

St. Teresa of Avila speaks of this as "the prayer of quiet" in which "[t]he faculties of the soul now retain only the power of occupying themselves wholly with God"; and at the same time, she declares, "it is possible to compose verse in order to give expression to the soul's joyful intoxication. God allows us to do two very different things simultaneously."[1] Such verses vary according to the ways the Spirit of God works within a person. These verses may at times be prophetic in expression and bring forth a word of wisdom or a word of knowledge. At other times they may resemble the *Psalms* and reflect either a joyful or sorrowful union with God.

It was in this way that King David wrote the *Psalms* through the inspiration of the Holy Spirit. David prayed for a new heart, and he found the key which leads directly to the Spirit and Heart of Christ, which contains *all* the hidden treasures of divine wisdom. Like David, we too should pray for purity of heart in order to have a greater knowledge of the Lord.

Seek to capture the heart of Christ for your very own. Our natural love alone is not adequate for loving God; we have to have a supernatural love in order to be accepted by the Father. Jesus alone knows what divine love is, and He alone can give the Father true worship, perfect sacrifice and total surrender. As the Sacred Heart of Jesus is the center of divine love, so our love can be divine if we are united to Him in His heart.

If a person had the heart of Christ (symbolic of His Holy Spirit, who is the Spirit of Love between the Father and Son), then he could love the Trinity with a divine love. Jesus' divine love was perfectly expressed in obedience unto death. Because His heart was perfect, His love was acceptable to the Father. Now, if Yahweh loved David the psalmist because his heart was good, just imagine how much more the Father loved Jesus, whose heart was perfect. If you are united in love to the heart of Christ, then your loving surrender to the Father will be acceptable, because in reality it would not be your human love He accepted, but the divine love of His Son.

How I earnestly desired to partake in Christ's total giving of self in order to be received by His Father in total acceptance. A simple sentence continually welled up within me as I sang day after day, "How can I love You with a love divine unless You give me Your heart (Spirit) for mine?" My whole being cried out, "Will that day ever come when my hopes are realized in Him?" And so I prayed and sang that which He gave me to sing, and my heart waited for the Lord. The following prayer in dialogue soon followed.

The Dialogue of Love

Give Me your heart
  so that your life becomes Mine; then
    the sacrifice is acceptable.

Give Me your blood
  in union with Mine so that
    the sacrifice is acceptable.

Give Me your soul
  in union with Mine so that
    I may be received.

Purify this victim in Your heart
    in the fire of Your divine love.

Let the fire of Love enkindle this victim
    until it is burning, until both flames are one
        in the sacrifice, unbloody, renewed.

Let the smoke from this victim become
    sweet and pleasing because
        it is united to Your Son.

Let the victim become transformed and become again
    through divine fire and love, the Son
        so that Christ lives in me,
        so that Christ dies in me,
        for the soul we both love.

To satisfy justice
    for this reason I was born, for this reason I die.
    So that He may reign in His beloved souls.

Don't you know I must be about My Father's business?

Let Me live:
    Die to yourself
        Let Me reign in your hearts!
                Amen.

These dialogues continued with the passing of time, and I knew the Lord was drawing me deeper into His Pascal Mystery through them. There were times when these conversations became prophetic words, but in my ignorance I was not able to comprehend their full significance until much later.

One such prophetic utterance came to my heart in 1957 in the form of a prayer petitioning the Lord to teach us the language of the Holy Spirit. That prayer was a foretelling of the outpouring which was soon to take place. It was a petition for the gift of praise, or the gift of tongues, commonly known as *glossiallia*. Now, there are those who do not believe in these gifts, but St. Paul exhorted the Church to pray in this way. "Surely, I should pray not only with the spirit but with the mind as well." (*1 Cor.* 14:15 TJB). Those who sing the praises of God by yielding to *glossiallia* are bringing forth the "word" and the strength of that empowered "word," for "Yah (God) is my STRENGTH, my SONG." (*Ex.* 15:2 TJB).

This spirit-filled song stirs up the gift of prophecy, brings forth the power of God to heal, activates the faith which produces miracles, and removes the heavy burden of sin. The *Psalms* of David reflected these very things, for intermingled with his praise of God is much prophecy. St. Paul cautioned the Church not to despise these things: "Be ambitious to prophesy, do not suppress the gift of tongues." (*1 Cor.* 14:39 TJB). The following is that prayer for *glossiallia* which gradually began to be fulfilled within the last decade or two with the Christian Community.

The Language of Charity

Jesus, teach us to speak the language of the Holy Spirit.
Teach us to speak the language of Charity
As the Blessed in Heaven do, who murmur not
But pour forth from their hearts the eloquence of Christ.
Giving to each other effusions of the beatitude of God,
Resulting in one celestial harmony of Love and Adoration.

Today when I attend the Charismatic Conferences and I see Spirit-filled Christians praising God, I understand what this "celestial harmony" is. Although the majority of these people have never studied music, the Spirit of God gives them the ability to sing and harmonize together. The Lord has fulfilled His word to those who keep His covenant when He said, "The people I have formed for myself will sing my praises." (*Is.* 43:21 TJB).

In Scripture we find many examples of this type of inspired praise. For instance, Hannah glorified the Lord by pouring out her heart in praise. (*Is.* 2:10 TJB). We also see the Spirit-filled Mary, the Mother of Christ, who when rejoicing in prophetic exultation sang the Magnificat (*Lk.* 1:46-55 TJB), and Zechariah, who sang the inspired Benedictus to God. (*Lk.* 1:67-79 TJB).

In all these Biblical characters we find a definite element of contemplative prayer; yet none of these people had been schooled in contemplative theology. They simply worshipped their God by yielding to His Spirit and externalizing their commitment in action. Martha's sister, Mary, arrived at contemplation by absorbing the life-giving words of Christ; Abraham received it by surrendering his will to God. Hannah and Zechariah were given this gift as they praised the Lord.

As you study the Covenant People, of the past or the present day, you come to notice a certain definite pattern or style evident in their worship. Individually or collectively, there is usually a word from God, which is followed by a response of prayer or inspired song, intermingled with prophecy, and accompanied by a complete acceptance of God's will. This spirit-filled prayer brings one into a profound depth of contemplation, resulting in a greater knowledge of the Lord or of some mystery of faith.

Those of you who aspire to contemplative prayer are urged to follow the Biblical pattern mentioned above. I learned from personal experience that profound encounters with the Lord can be realized by using these procedures. But notice also that the people just mentioned went through their daily tasks with this song in their hearts. That spiritual song, which required no mental effort, enabled them to focus their inner beings continually upon the Lord. In this way, they were always in the Presence of the Lord.

Noah was another Spirit-led person who quietly listened to God's direction as he worked conscientiously building the Ark. Can you imagine St. Joseph, the guardian of the young Christ, laboring at his carpenter's trade while his heart and mind were focused upon the Son of God? Imagine the Mother of Christ baking bread while pondering the mysteries of God within her heart. St. Teresa of Avila tells us that she was able to cook eggs while contemplating the Lord, thereby giving homemakers an insight into the possibilities of profound prayer. All these people lived busy lives within the world, yet this in no way hindered their union with God. Their example should be an incentive to all Christians. These opportunities of profound prayer are open to all God's people regardless of their environment. Each person has the potential to evolve spiritually unto the perfection that God has called him to through the power of His Spirit. You have but to yield to the Spirit of Christ.

The examples of these faithful people of God encouraged me to seek the Lord throughout the day. One day while washing dishes, I was praying mentally to the Lord, and through the activity of His Spirit I began to receive a song and vision simultaneously. As the words began to form, I saw the pitiful form of the crucified Christ nailed to the Cross, His blood dripping from His pierced hands onto the parched earth beneath the Cross. Looking upon this barren ground, I recalled the words that God had said to Adam and Eve: "Cursed be the ground because of you! For you are dirt, and to dirt you shall return." (*Gen.* 3:17, 19 NAB).

Like a dry sponge, this cursed ground soaked up the blood of its Savior in a hungry plea for redemption. Numb with grief, I stood there watching this ignominious scene unfold, the supreme sacrifice of God's Son seemingly wasted upon this desolate earth. Then the earth shifted, moved, and began to take different forms as the Spirit moved to fashion the shapes of millions of people from this blood-red, redeemed earth. These earthen people were placed around the crucified Christ. They were lifeless; but, as His blood flowed upon them from the Cross, they lifted up their arms in praise and reached out to their source of life. They stirred, slowly; and giving evidence of His Spirit acting within, their voices, like silver trumpets, shouted out the celestial praises of their Redeemer. Their voices resounded with triumphant joy, and the sound of it grew as loud as thunder, filling the whole earth. As Christ's sacrificed life diminished, their recreated lives increased in vigor. His Spirit flowed through them now, and these redeemed people encircled their Lord and continuously praised Him. The vision vanished, but the words continued in my heart.

Years later I found these words in Scripture which were almost identical to the vision the Lord had given: "Then I heard what sounded like the shouts of a great crowd, or the roaring of the deep, or mighty peals of thunder, as they cried: Alleluia! The Lord is King, our God, the Almighty! For this is the wedding day of the Lamb: His bride has prepared herself for the wedding." (*Rev.* 19:6,7 NAB). These thousands of people were raised up and given new life through the blood of the Lamb and through His Spirit.

This prophetic vision and word took place three years before the great outpouring of the Spirit on the people of God in the 1960's and 70's. I rejoice as I see thousands upon thousands of these redeemed and hear their victorious song of praise at Charismatic Conferences. Praise God!

At the time of this vision the following song was also received, and it foretold the renewal and the era of evangelism which is now breaking forth over the entire earth. I had never heard of the "born again experience," yet the Spirit inspired me to title it so. The song was written in the singular, to Israel, as the covenant son and as a nation of God's people.

Rebirth in the Lord

The Holy Spirit came to you
And turned the darkness into Light.
Sparks of Fire pierced you through;
Burning lamps within the new-born Life

Raged through your soul, burning bright,
Magnified your vision of the Lord.
You saw so clearly. You knew His Will.
Son of God someday you'd be.

He sent His holy spouse Mary to see
If the measurements were just right —
The perfection of Jesus you must be
To fit that tree, that barren tree.

It needed a victim to fulfill
The Passion of our Jesus Lord.
Mary was pleased; you fit the bill.
But, oh, what a dark, what a stormy night!

The Cross awaits you; the lance is thrust.
Your blood flows freely, absorbed by the dust —
With out-stretched arms — in a silent cry
Voices rise so loud, thunder shakes the sky.

"We were dead; now we live because of Thee.
You loved man enough, it's plain to see.
You chose to be nailed to the Paradise Tree."

The story hasn't ended yet, my friends.
Time completes what must be.
A desolate dove sings of its Love;
"Please, dear God, set me free.
The night is still dark, and I cannot see;
The bars of my flesh are a prison to me."

Soon the dawn of the soul begins to glow,
And in the night there comes a great Light —
The Master is here. He calls you by name,
"Child of God"; there isn't another the same.

"Enter in, prince of Heaven, son of the King;
Well done, faithful servant. Here's your reward,
My son, My son," saith the Lord.

Now, prophetic words such as these are not always easy to comprehend, because they are not fulfilled immediately; sometimes years pass by before one can see the total picture. In many instances these things do not come to pass even within one's lifetime. Yet God will bring them about; for He never speaks an idle word, but faithfully sees to it that His word comes to fruition.

Can you now see how the prayer of contemplation cuts through preconceived barriers of time and place, and that God does indeed speak to those who sincerely seek Him with all their hearts? Who would ever have believed that such profound prayer can take place while doing the most menial tasks, such as washing dishes or cooking a meal? It happened to Moses while he was herding sheep. So, we understand then that there is no insignificant time or place for the Lord. You do not always have to be on your knees, but your heart must be ever ready to receive His word. You must not only open your heart to that word, but you must of necessity respond to it, for His word gives life. No other word is capable of giving and sustaining life except the Word of God.

As I have said, at times the words which the Lord speaks within our hearts come to us in the form of three locutions. The Jesuit, Augustine Poulain describes these various manifestations.

1. The exterior or auricular locutions are heard by the ear...
2. Imaginative locutions also composed by the foregoing can be said to be received by the imaginative sense. They, with those that come after them, are included in the term "interior locutions."
3. Intellectual locutions. This is a simple communication of thought without words, and consequently without the use of any definite language.[2]

It is important to recognize locutions in order not to lose the precious gift of God's words to us. But locutions were but one means of communication that the Lord used. He began to teach me others, for I was as yet ignorant of His ways.

Once during Holy Week, while I was receiving the Sacrament of Penance, He spoke a prophetic word which I related to the priest. The priest recognized this as a movement of the Spirit and was himself deeply moved. It overwhelmed me because I was spiritually immature, yet we must listen to the teachings in Scripture which say, "Do not stifle the Spirit. Do not despise prophecies. Test everything; retain what is good." (*1 Thess.* 5:19-21 NAB).

From that time on I was able to discern the voice of my Shepherd when He spoke prophetically. Jesus Himself declared, "The sheep hear his voice... The sheep follow him because they recognize his voice... They will not follow a stranger; such a one they will flee, because they do not recognize a stranger's voice." (*Jn.* 10:3-5 NAB). In 1972, the Spirit prompted me to write to Rome about some prophecies, and much to my surprise I received a kind letter in response.

At that time there were no doors opened for laypeople to minister within the Church. The Lord was doing a new thing, and the avant garde was having a rough time of it. Persecutions and trials became my daily bread. An atmosphere of doubt began to surround me as I walked hesitantly over the hot sands of uncertainty, but the Lord permitted me to pass through these trials unharmed. Earnestly seeking His will in prayer, I received these words: "Get up now, and stand on your feet. I have appeared to you to designate you as my servant and as a witness to what you have seen of me and what you will see of me." (*Acts* 26:16 NAB).

Now that I trusted in the Lord, my doubts faded into oblivion, and the assurance of His love was like a protective shield around me. I knew that I was not alone as I walked on toward the distant horizon. The future held out its hand, beckoning me to see what God had prepared from the foundation of the world for those who are faithful to Him. And as my journey toward the Father progressed, He continued to teach me things I had never dreamed possible. The remainder of this book relates some of these teachings and encounters.

–3–

Sharing in His Fruitfulness

In Biblical days God would personally choose individuals to serve as His stewards and ministers. As in the case of Samuel the prophet, He often called them by name. At other times, as in the life of Noah and Abraham, He would call by speaking a directive word. In still other cases, He would arouse a great desire within their hearts to seek Him, as in the case of Moses and others. Now, in the New Testament, it is Jesus who chooses people through whom He will impart fruitfulness. Although He is now in glory, He continues to empower us with the spiritual gifts necessary to bring forth His Kingdom. He stressed the fact that He expects His servants to bear fruit. "You did not choose me," He said, "No, I chose you; and I commissioned you to go out and to bear fruit, fruit that will last." (*Jn.* 15:16 TJB).

Now, one cannot bear His fruit unless one abides on the heavenly Vine, which is Jesus. Unless one lives in Him, all human effort will result in failure, for He said, "Apart from me you can do nothing." (*Jn.* 15:5 NAB).

Furthermore, we see that the apparent fruitfulness of our good works is nothing less than the activity of the Holy Spirit dwelling within us, for it is written, "All your fruitfulness comes from me." (*Hosea* 14:19 TJB). We become more fruitful then, according to the degree that we submit our own activity to the Spirit's direction. Our prayer should be, "Lord, increase Your Presence within us." Our attitude should be that of one who is willing to be molded into that which He desires. "The people I have formed for myself," He said, "will sing my praise" (*Is.* 43:21 TJB). He is now in the process of forming a People who will praise Him and who by their praise become the fruitful trees whose roots absorb the sweet rain of the Spirit.

Remember the time when Jesus cursed the fig tree because it bore no fruit (M*att.* 21:18-20 TJB)? Can you recall the story about the servant who hid his talents while his master was away, and later, how that servant was cast into darkness (*Matt.* 25:14-30 TJB)? These are not soft words! These admonitions are like so many fiery arrows aimed at those unprofitable servants who neglect to use the gifts which He lavishly bestowed. In no uncertain terms has Jesus demonstrated the fact that He has come to serve and that His people are to follow His example and bring forth spiritual fruit. They are to bring forth a spiritual harvest of souls for the Kingdom. The unprofitable have no excuse, nor can they plead ignorance. They have been told!

The Lord of Harvests does not discriminate in His choice of laborers. He makes provision for even the weakest of men by giving of His own strength in order that His designs be accomplished. What great wisdom He has! Today, even as of old, He continues to use the weak in the world to confound the proud so that no man may glory except in the Lord Jesus.

Thus, because I believed in His word, I had no choice but to strive faithfully to fulfill the spiritual directive which each moment brought to me. But I was also confident that in whatever circumstance He placed me, I could draw upon His strength to bring His word to fruition.

In time I found myself ministering to others in ways which astounded me. This ministry brought me into contact with people who had a wide range of needs, but just so the Spirit opened a variety of charismatic gifts to aid me. I seemed to be especially drawn to those with spiritual needs. These hungering souls spoke with a fluency that needed no words.

Within a whirlwind of encounters, I recall in particular a man named Amos who lived in the jungle of the inner city. He was known as a "hard core" inmate who had recently been released from a long confinement within the state prison. I met him while he was standing with a group of young people who had agreed to attend a talk and film about the Lord. During the film, I heard muffled sobs coming from Amos, and I knew that his heart had been touched. As he tried to stop crying, he asked me, "Why hadn't anyone told me about Jesus before?"

This was 20th-Century America — were my ears deceiving me? Surely everyone in this land of freedom and opportunity had heard about the Christ. But to my amazement, I learned that Amos was not the only one within this "enlightened" society who had never heard about the Son of God. Multiply this ignorance thousands of times within the larger cities and tell me what you think. How desolate! An expanse of hungering souls seeking some purpose for their creation. Where are the missionaries, the evangelists, the preachers and teachers? Where are they? Surely this is missionary territory. And yet, we send missionaries abroad who cannot speak the language of the people. Why do we not send the English-speaking missionaries into our own cities? Who will bring these people back to God? Whom will you send, Lord? Our need is overwhelming, Lord. Send laborers into our cities.

Amos was more than anxious to learn more about the "Man" who loved him enough to die for him. He had not believed that such love was possible, yet here sacrificial love was proven. One night as we spoke about the Lord, Amos began to pour out his bitter life story. Neglect and abuse were all he had known since the time he was very, very young. And his adolescent years were spent in reform school. His grief cried out to Heaven for healing and compassion. Amos cried for Baptism, and he received the Christ as Lord. Christ was the one to heal the scars of neglect, abuse, and sin. Amos grew like a beautiful wildflower under the nourishing rays of the Son.

When you watch God radically change a man like Amos, you see that the power of redemption is real; and the immensity of it all is frightening, because it makes you perceive the majesty of God. I stood silently by, observing the Lord recreate a hard-core criminal into a new creature in Christ, and that is overwhelming! Amos became a star witness for the Lord in the dark city, and the darkness gave way to new light.

Once I had seen the renewing power of God, I longed to share it with my children, but I wondered if they were too young to understand the meaning of a personal Pentecost. It was time to find out. One day the Spirit prompted me to speak to them about surrendering their lives to Him as Lord and about the baptism of the Holy Spirit. After our chat, one child stepped out in faith and said that she would like to receive this outpouring. She renewed her baptismal vows, and as we laid hands upon her she began to shed tears of joy as the gift of tongues was given to her. Then, each one in turn stepped forward as we gave praise to God. What a grace-filled day that was, when each person accepted the Holy Spirit's anointing. We celebrated together the whole day.

Then one evening during night prayers, one child was quietly reflecting when suddenly she burst into tears. Something unusual had happened. Having led her into another room, I asked her what was wrong. "Oh, Mommy," she said, "I saw Jesus in the room while we were praying." Now this child knew nothing about visions; she stated simply what had happened. The effects of this encounter were a great blessing for her.

We found that our faith was rewarded for obeying the words of Scripture which state, "If you, then who are evil, know how to give your children what is good, how much more will your Father in heaven give good things to those who ask him!" (*Matt.* 7:11 TJB). Before long the various gifts of the Holy Spirit began to manifest themselves within the family circle. The children were favored with utterance of prophecy and healings that would take place. Children have a way of responding to God that is as natural as breathing, and we would do well to imitate them in their docility. This spiritual innocence is the criterion for entrance into the Kingdom, for Jesus said: "Let the children come to me and do not hinder them. For it is to such as these that the kingdom of God belongs." (*Mk.* 10:14 TJB).

Who are these children of the Kingdom? The Word tells us who they are: "Everyone moved by the Spirit is a son of God. The spirit you received . . . is the spirit of sons . . . The Spirit himself bears witness that we are children of God." (*Rom.* 8:15-16 TJB). Although they are not aware of the great graces they are receiving, with the help of adults the Spirit-filled child can develop into a spiritual giant. We can all pray, but it is the Lord who will give growth to these little ones.

We found that the more we witnessed, the more doors began to open for ministry. Our stewardship was not always easy, for the persecutions increased in proportion to the blessings which were given. As we yielded to the Holy Spirit in all situations, we found that He continued to confirm our words with His deeds. Although we had been active within our Church for years, we found in our service to others a deeper satisfaction, as we knew this to be the will of God. We had often discussed the idea that we thought the Lord had for a long time been preparing us to do a work for Him. We realized that the Lord was doing something new in the world by pouring out His Holy Spirit. We recalled the time when Pope John XXIII had prayed for a new Pentecost within the Church, and the result of his prayer is evidently taking place within our lifetimes.

In time we began to have prayer meetings at home. Many people came from the surrounding towns, from many parishes and from different denominations. At these meetings the Lord moved in a tremendous way. Several people were healed of cancer. There was one particular prayer meeting which stands out in our memory. On that night, the praises of the Lord seemed particularly strong. Then we all heard a great thunderclap. It felt as if the building had been struck by lightning, but there were no clouds in the sky. Immediately afterwards, most of us experienced being slain in the Spirit, or resting in the Lord. This sometimes happens when the outpouring of the Holy Spirit is very strong. No one alone had ministered here; rather, it was the Lord who had worked within the heart of each separate person. Everyone there was profoundly aware of the Presence of the Lord. A young football coach was so "drunk" in the Spirit that he could not stand or sit. He later told us, with tears streaming down his face, that as he surrendered his life to the Lord, he experienced the infilling of the Spirit from his feet to the top of his head. It was not long before the Lord began to use him to bring many young people to Himself.

There were times when the Lord would speak a word of knowledge to us or a word of wisdom. Once He told us to visit a prominent clergyman in our area who was critically ill in order to pray for his healing. We hesitated at first, but our doubts were soon overcome and we did our best to see him. We held him up in prayer continuously. Two months later we received yet another word concerning him. The Lord said, "Continue your prayers for him. I will heal him. Do not doubt Me. I will heal him." Shortly thereafter, the clergyman had greatly improved. Some months later the word of knowledge came again: "He is now completely healed." It has been five years now, and this man enjoys good health. We praised God for His goodness.

I searched for teaching concerning prophetic words and how to discern the authenticity of such words. I was satisfied with the teaching of the Jesuit scholar Poulain, who wrote: "Can we ever be certain that a revelation made to another person is purely divine? Yes. For the Old Testament prophets furnished indubitable signs of their mission. Otherwise they would not have been believed. . . A prophecy fulfilled will be the equivalent of a miracle if it was couched in definitive language and could not have been the result of chance or the conjecture of the Devil."[1]

The prophetic words which we had received fell into this category; thus we knew for certain that their source was the Lord. Because they were received as interior words, they could not have been given through the influence of evil entities. We realized that it is extremely important to discern any prophetic word correctly lest people be deceived by false prophecy and lead others astray.

As you can see, the revelational gifts, such as a word of knowledge or wisdom, or prophecy, are valuable tools which help the people of God to understand the mind of the Lord in dealing with particular situations. The true prophetic word then becomes the guideline of the Spirit's activity. These word-gifts are, in a special way, the sign posts leading the contemplative closer to his goal. Three of the gifts: knowledge, understanding, and wisdom, unite in a special manner in contemplation.

All theologians recognize the gifts of understanding and wisdom as the principles which call forth contemplation. . .[2]

These gifts are usually given to those who are spiritually mature. The Lord does not intend that such gifts be abused, and He will not give these spiritual tools to those who do not know how to make good use of them. Many times people who do not have charismatic discernment attempt to judge the operation of these revelational gifts with human knowledge. Such judgments can cause great harm within a body of Christians. The gifts of the Spirit must be discerned by spiritual means, and only the spiritual man can understand them.

The mature in Christ, regardless of their worldly positions or their state in life, should be given the opportunity to discern and use the gifts which the Lord has given them for the benefit of the Christian community. Truth alone must reign supreme in the acceptance or rejection of prophetic words. The Lord's standards are different than the world's standards, and those who follow Him must of necessity be diligent in seeking His will. We must therefore have circumcised hearts in order to receive the plenitude of the fruitful action of God's Spirit.

The Lord began to teach me discernment through personal experiences relating to the Sacraments. As time progressed, I discerned the knowledge He instilled within my spirit in still other situations.

For example, while attending a conference at Notre Dame University some years ago, I heard a young man speak, and immediately I recognized the voice of the Lord, for "the sheep . . . know his voice . . . .They do not recognize the voice of strangers." (*Jn.* 10:3,5 TJB). I wrote down the special words of prophecy and was inspired to send them to Rome. I felt that this was the Lord's will, and He confirmed it. I did not expect a response, but within two weeks I received a kind letter.

The Lord slowly erased any misgivings we might have had about our ministry and increased our faith so that we understood the way in which we should go. The Spirit of God was leading and supporting us even as He said, "I will instruct you and show you the way you should walk." (*Ps.* 32:8 NAB). We had many needs, and we had no alternative but to ask the Father for His assistance. We found that praying in the Spirit was truly a fruitful prayer before the throne of God.

Several years ago the Lord gave us a sure sign of His providence in a situation which seemed impossible. A friend and I were returning home from Michigan after a Renewal Conference and we were caught in the worst blizzard since 1890. We crept along at a snail's pace past thousands of cars stranded along the highway. My friend insisted that we continue through this snowstorm, which blanketed everything in white. About halfway home my companion excitedly said, "Look at the windshield! Can you see what's happening?" She started to laugh in disbelief. "Look! The snow isn't touching the car or the windows!" This seemed impossible, but our eyes were not deceiving us. This raging blizzard was dropping down tons of snow, but our car remained untouched for the space of a half hour. The snow would blow toward us and come within a foot or two of the automobile, and then turn in the opposite direction. We even turned the windshield wipers off. We did not need them, for the Presence of the Lord was shielding us from the storm. What more could He do to show us His love? Yes, Lord, we believe. "God our shield, now look on us and be kind to your anointed." (*Ps.* 84:9 TJB). The following letter is the personal testimony of my companion in the storm.

To Whom It May Concern:

I, Dorothy Jurus of Struthers, Ohio, witnessed the event of the snow blizzard which is described in this book. I was the friend who was described in this story as driving the car. This story is true as it is represented here, and I want to personally testify to it for the glory of God. The Lord heard our prayers and gave us His divine protection.

Sincerely,
Dorothy Jurus
246 W. Hopewell Dr.
Struthers, Ohio 44471

This incident reminded me of how Shadrach, Meshack, and Abednego were able to live in the midst of a raging fire. They were saved from the elements by praising the creations of the King: "Fire and heat! Bless the Lord; give glory and eternal praise to him." (*Dan.* 3:66 TJB). We followed their example by praising God for the snow. "Ice and snow!" we sang, "Bless the Lord; give glory and eternal praise to him." (*Dan.* 3:70 TJB). The inanimate snow thereby gave glory to God as He responded to our prayers. Once more the storm around the Lord's people had been quieted. The prayer of praise was the key that turned the threatening storm into a time of glory for the Lord. "Deliver us by your wonders, and bring glory to your name, O Lord." (*Dan.* 3:43 NAB). Every creature, animate and inanimate, must humbly submit to the Lord of glory. Do you see how He uses every situation to increase our faith? With grateful hearts we raised our voices in songs of thanksgiving.

The Lord was indeed teaching and bringing to light many things which we had read about, but had never experienced. Now we were beginning to experience the fulfillment of His words. Like so many others, we never hoped or expected that this would happen to us. The Spirit was moving, and the words kept ringing in our ears, "Anything you ask in my name I will do." (*Jn.* 14:14 NAB).

The Sword of the Spirit

–4–

Mystical Union with Mary

In this book I have tried to show the reader some of the avenues of prayer which are open to us in order to attain the highest possible union with God. Spiritual union with Mary is one of these ways; yet, there are people, even among the religious, who do not truly understand what this is. When I refer to this union as "mystic," I do not want to confuse the reader. Often this word is misused and associated in the wrong sense with the occult or false mysticism. This is not what I am writing about. I am speaking here of a very high level of spiritual union with the Holy Spirit of God through Mary.

By meditating on the Word of God, I have come to see that, long before she was born of flesh, Mary was spiritually conceived in the mind of God. In *Genesis*, we read that when God spoke to the serpent about the Woman, He was referring to Mary: "I will put enmity between you and the woman and between your offspring and hers." (*Gen.* 3:15 NAB). We also find references to Mary in symbolic terms in later scriptural history. For example, "She is a tree of life to those who grasp her." (*Prov.* 3:18 NAB). St. Louis M. DeMontfort and St. Alphonsus also refer to Mary as this "tree of life": "Mary is everywhere the veritable tree who bears the Fruit of life, and the Mother who produces it.[1] Whoever desires the fruit must go to the tree..."[2]

Not only is the Virgin Mary known as the Tree of Life, she is also called the Seat of Wisdom and the Bride in liturgical prayer.

I believe that God has a special plan for His holy Mother among the people of God which has not yet been realized. Since Mary was so special to God, she should also be very special to God's people. Let us strive to grasp the significance of God's relationship to the favored woman.

We read that the angel Gabriel, who was sent to Mary, proclaimed, "Rejoice, O highly favored daughter! The Lord is with you. Blessed are you among women." (*Lk*. 1:28 NAB). Then Gabriel told her that she would conceive and bear a Son, to be named Jesus. Mary could not understand how this could happen, since she knew no man. The angel answered her: "The Holy Spirit will come upon you; hence, the holy offspring to be born will be called the Son of God." (*Lk*. 1:35 NAB). At the moment when she responded, "Let it be done," Mary became *wedded* to God's Spirit in a permanent, eternal way.

Since the Holy Spirit is permanently united to Mary's spirit, we discover that when we honor Mary we are simultaneously honoring the Holy Spirit, who dwells within her. The Holy Spirit has entered into Mary as into His own personal paradise. "I have come to my garden, my sister, my bride." (*Sg. of Sg*. 5:1 NAB). Mary was God's special paradise; she brought forth the Fruit of God. She is also called the Bride of the Lord and a Fountain of living water. "You are an enclosed garden, my sister, my bride, an enclosed garden, a fountain sealed." (*Sg. of Sg*. 4:12 NAB). She is a fountain because she contains the Source of the Living Water, the Spirit. As the Lord delighted in making Mary His Mother, He also wishes us to delight in accepting her spiritual Motherhood ourselves.

To give ourselves to Jesus through Mary is to imitate God the Father, who has given us His Son only through Mary, and who communicated to God the Son, who has come to us only through Mary, and who, by giving us an example, told us "that as He has done so you must also do." (*Jn*. 13:15). . . . Is it not fitting, asks St. Bernard, that grace should return to its Author by the same channel which conveyed it to us?[3]

This is one of the most profound statements on the example of the Blessed Trinity and Their relationship with Mary that I have ever read. One cannot go wrong by following its advice. Jesus showed us the desire of His heart when, dying on the Cross, He said, "There is your mother." (*Jn.* 19:27 NAB). St. John the Evangelist, who represented God's people as the Beloved, received Mary according to the words of Jesus and took her home as his Mother. As I meditated upon the Book of Wisdom, I saw that this was prophesied already by the author of that book. It was not a case of Mary needing a house or protection, for God would provide for her needs. Rather, it was another step in God's plan to establish Mary in her role as the Spiritual Mother of those who were adopted "sons of God." This fits the description which Scripture gives of Mary and St. John, who was the youngest of the disciples.

So I determined to take her to live with me, knowing that she would be my counselor while all was well, and my comfort in care and grief. For her sake I should have glory among the masses, and esteem from the elders, though I be but a youth. (*Wis.* 8:9, 10 NAB).

St. John the Evangelist, in receiving Mary, became her first spiritual son, the first of the new order where she is the New Eve and the Mother of us all. All who obey Jesus as St. John did will be born into the family of God.

As the Holy Ghost has espoused Mary and has produced in her, by her and from her, His masterpiece, Jesus Christ, the Word Incarnate, and has never repudiated His spouse, so now He continues to produce the elect in her and by her, in a mysterious but real manner.[4]

It was in the Book of Wisdom that I found many descriptions of Mary. This book was written by an unknown prophet who lived with the Jewish community exiled in Egypt. Through meditation, the Holy Spirit gave me to understand that the verses were prophetic descriptions of our own union with Mary. Is it just a coincidence that Mary, being the Seat of Wisdom, taught St. John the mysteries of the Divine Family and a profound knowledge; is it any wonder that St. John received the greatest outpouring of the gifts of Wisdom after he had accepted Mary as a spiritual Mother? "Yet all good things together came to me in her company, and countless riches at her hands." (*Wis.* 7:11 NAB). "For she is the instructress in the understanding of God." (*Wis.* 8:4 NAB).

Because of his obedience to Jesus, St. John was given the word of Wisdom in greater measure than any other man. Solomon, in the Old Testament, had wisdom in administrative ability which helped him to acquire wealth. But St. John had a far superior wisdom and wealth, allowing him vision into Heaven itself and a keen knowledge of the mysteries of faith.

At the end of his life, Solomon lost his inheritance because "when Solomon was old his wives had turned his heart to strange gods, and his heart was not entirely with the Lord." (*1 Kgs.* 11:4 NAB). His heart was divided and his spirit became lukewarm. Because of this, he lost the gifts God had bestowed upon him. "So the Lord said to Solomon: 'Since this is what you want, and you have not kept my covenant and my statutes which I enjoined on you, I will deprive you of the kingdom and give it to your servant." (*1Kgs.* 11:11 NAB). This will happen to all those who do not keep the covenant; they eventually will lose the Kingdom of God.

St. John, on the other hand, inherited Wisdom through his obedience to the God-Man, Christ Jesus, and he gained wisdom through Mary, his new Mother. For "Now I was a well-favored child" (*Wis.* 8:19 NAB) "and rejoiced in them all, because Wisdom is their leader, though I had not known that she is the mother of these." (*Wis.* 7:12 NAB). Furthermore, St. John loved the Trinity and the Mother of Jesus above all else. His obedient response to the word of Christ released the power that transformed John into an adopted son of God; likewise, "all who are led by the Spirit of God are the sons of God." (*Rom.* 8:14 NAB). We see from the words of St. Augustine that a man becomes the image of what he loves most: If he loves earth, he becomes earth; if he loves God, he becomes like God. If he loves Mary, he becomes her son; that is, another Jesus.[5]

The spiritual transformation that took place in St. John's life is also meant to take place within each believer. Our prayer, as that of the prophets before us, should be: "Give me Wisdom, the attendant at your throne, and reject me not from among your children; for I am your servant, the son of your handmaid." (*Wis.* 9:4 NAB). Who is the handmaid of the Lord? It is none other than Mary, who proclaimed, "I am the handmaid of the Lord, let what you have said be done to me." (*Lk.* 1:38 NAB). St. John was the first spiritual son of Mary, and he did indeed receive the profound wisdom which he wrote about in the Book of Revelation.

Like St. John, we should receive the Blessed Mother into our hearts, for she "enters the soul of the Lord's servant." (*Wis.* 10:16

NAB). When we receive Mary as our spiritual Mother, the Holy Spirit comes and abides with us. This spiritual union bears fruit in the new birth of a spiritual son, who will be transformed gradually into the new likeness of Christ; that is, if he continues to be faithful to God.

It is this unity which exists between Mary's spirit and the Holy Spirit that is the basis of what is called the "mystical union" with Mary. It can be the first step in acquiring great knowledge of the person of Christ, since Mary was the one who knew every little detail of His life from birth to death. Who upon earth knew Him better, served Him more, or shared His life more intimately? We must go to her and ask her to teach us about her Son. For a deeper understanding of the unitive life with Mary, I suggest a prayerful reading of St. Louis DeMonfort's work, and in particular, his book, *True Devotion to Mary.*

This mystical union with Mary has been experienced by many who have recorded their experiences. Among them are St. Mary of St. Teresa; St. Symeon, the Byzantine theologian; and the World War II martyr, Saint Maximillian Kolbe. Mary of Teresa explains, "There is sometimes shown and given to me a life of the spirit in Our Lady, a rest, enjoyment, fusion, union in and with her..."

When my spirit is turned to God in all simplicity, nakedness and tranquillity, resting in His Being without images by contemplation of that absolute Being, my soul experiences at the same time a union with and blossoming in Mary inasmuch as she is united with God; so much that they seem to be but one object. . . .

But very few people know this life both for and in Mary and for and in God experimentally, for it is given only to some of her true lovers...

When the Eternal Father sends into our hearts the spirit of His Son crying, "Abba! Father!" .

...then the spirit of the Son produces the same effect in relation to dear Mother ... crying, "Mother!" There is only one spirit, the spirit of Christ, that arouses in our souls this love for and life in Mary, as it arouses love for and life in God, and both according to the manner in which they were realized in our Lord Jesus Christ.[6]

This unitive prayer with Mary can only be accomplished by responding to the word of God as He speaks to the heart. The

Blessed Mother always responded to that word and did His will perfectly, and because of her all creation was blessed. When she pronounced her "fiat" to the Lord, a Trinitarian relationship was established with the Woman.

When he explicated the parable in *Matthew* 22:1-4, St. Symeon wrote about the role of Mary as the Bride and as a vessel which God would use to convey His life.

The Heavenly Father is the king in this parable, says Symeon. But who is getting married? It is His Son, Jesus Christ. And we note it is a question not of one marriage, but of many marriages.

The first spouse of the Father's Son is Mary, all-pure Virgin. In the Annunciation the Word by the Holy Spirit entered immanently yet physically into her womb. Such is then the indescribable union that is the mystical marriage with God.

But what happened to the Virgin Mary happens also in a series of mystical marriages where . . . in each of the faithful and the sons of the Day there is produced continually the same marriage in an analogous way and without great difference.

Jesus Christ is conceived within the Christian mystic; not corporeally, as Mary the Mother of God so conceived, but spiritually and substantially (*pneumatikos men ousiodos*). We conceive the Word of God in our hearts, if we maintain in us our soul virgin and pure.[7]

Jesus is continually engendered in us through the same vessel which gave Him flesh.

We are also told that Saint Maximillian Kolbe had experienced mystical union with Mary. He dreamt of evangelizing the world for Christ with the Immaculata, that is, by working as an instrument in her hands . . . always guided by the interior vision of faith he had through mystic union with his Queen in the Holy Spirit.[8]

By their union with Mary and the Holy Spirit, these persons experienced new life and power in Christ as adopted sons of God. They understood the meaning of these words: "Happy is the man who listens to me, who day after day watches at my gates to guard the portals. For the man who finds me finds life, he will win favor from Yahweh." (*Prov.* 8:34 NAB).

By standing upon these words of Scripture, we will find life in and through Mary, who points the way to Christ, and we will begin to grasp God's Wisdom. I have experienced this mystic union with

Mary, for "she is my instructress in the understanding of God, the selector of his works." (*Wis.* 8:4 NAB). Previously I had almost no understanding of the ways of God; but when I accepted Mary as my heavenly Mother, the Book of Knowledge was opened, and I learned much about Christ and the Holy Spirit.

Before this union, I had accepted God as my loving Father; yet, through inspiration, I felt that I should also ask Mary to be my Mother. I could not foresee the result, but I felt the Lord moving me even closer to Himself. Marvels began to occur for me once I had accepted His direction, "There is your Mother." It does not dishonor God, nor diminish His glory in any way to honor Mary. In fact, it increases His glory, for no one loves Him as Mary does.

It was on May 18, 1963, the anniversary of my mother's death, that I began to reflect upon Mary, my heavenly Mother. I would dwell upon Mary's many privileges and God's love for her. This was the Woman who would co-operate in all His designs. She was in His mind from the time of Creation. His love for her drew Him to earth, as He had chosen her to bear His only begotten Son. "You are all-beautiful, my beloved, and there is no blemish in you." (*Sg. of Sg.* 4:7). "As a lily among thorns, so is my beloved among women." (*Sg. of Sg.* 2:2 NAB). Do you see how graciously the Spirit of God directed men to write about His Bride? This delicate, young, Jewish girl was to bear the Savior of the World and provide for the Son of God. What an awesome task! Yet her soul trusted in God, who loved her above all others. For "one alone is my dove, my perfect one." (*Sg. of Sg.* 6:9 NAB).

Because Mary believed, that which might seem impossible became a reality. Because she responded to the Spirit, she was overshadowed by Him. "Before I knew it, my heart had made me the blessed one of my kinswomen." (*Sg. of Sg.* 6:12 NAB). What a joyful excitement Mary must have felt as she hastened to visit Elizabeth, at whose house she sang God's praises with exultation. "Wisdom sings her own praises, before her own people she proclaims her glory." (*Sirach* 24:1 NAB). In her jubilant Magnificat, Mary prophesied the role enjoined upon her by the Spirit. "For he has looked upon his servant in her lowliness: all ages to come shall call me blessed. God who is mighty has done great things for me, holy is his name." (*Lk.* 1:48,49 NAB).

What great yearning and anticipation filled the heart of Mary at that time. To have the Source of all life living within you! What ecstasy that must have been. Each movement of the Christ-child must have caused her to be consumed by the flaming fulfillment of divine love within her. This holy, but still human, temple of the King of Kings would surely have perished of sheer love if her beloved Lord had not sustained her by His power. Surely this divine love of God for Mary had the sweetness and intoxication of spiced wine, though in reality it was the inflowing of the Spirit of God. God Himself became the source of her strength, for "God who is mighty has done great things for me." (*Lk.* 1:49 NAB).

While I was meditating upon this, the Lord granted me the grace of contemplation, and thus I received an interior vision of the Mother of Jesus. She seemed to be about sixteen years old and had delicate, refined features. She was slim and of average height. Her brown, wavy hair hung loosely about her radiant face. On her head was a white, transparent veil. Mary was so outstanding in beauty and grace that no woman could begin to compare with her. She was truly the "most beautiful among women." (*Sg. of Sg.* 5:9 NAB). She was holding the Infant in her left arm with His face toward her shoulder. The Messiah was wrapped in white swaddling cloth bound by a thin ribbon. In silence and in wonder I gazed upon her; I was dazzled by her beauty. Her eyes looked directly into mine, and they were the most beautiful I had ever seen. From her face streamed rays of transparent light like moonbeams or sunbeams. She smiled. Her lips were like rose petals, which parted to speak. She said one word which contains all else—the living word— "Jesus." Her voice was melodious, and all about her I heard a heavenly symphony. Although I could not perceive them, I knew that some heavenly Court was attending upon her and the Infant. When she spoke, I could smell an exotic perfume. Years later, I discovered this passage: "Your name spoken is a spreading of perfume." (*Sg. of Sg.* 1:3 NAB).

Soon she approached. Even as I thought it, I knew that her spirit had passed into mine. "And passing into holy souls from age to age, she produces friends of God and prophets." (*Wis.* 7:27 NAB). She wished to convey to me her love for the infant King. She gave me the Babe to hold in my arms; as she did, I felt as if I never wanted to put Him down. Oh, how could anyone lay Him down even to sleep, this Almighty One? Like all of those united in God's Spirit, Mary and I were united in mind and heart; she taught me her own sentiments. I would hold the Child caressingly every minute. My heart was so overjoyed that I wanted to dance with her Babe in my arms. Like David, who danced around the Ark of the Covenant, so did my feet want to leap for shear joy! St. Mechtilde writes about this spiritual dance; she says,

> I cannot dance, O Lord, unless Thou lead me.
> If Thou wilt that I leap joyfully
> Thou must Thyself first dance and sing!
> — Then will I leap for love
> From love to knowledge
> From knowledge to fruition
> From fruition to beyond all human sense...[9]

I held these sentiments within my heart as I looked upon this heavenly Child. I knew that every word from Mary to Him was perfect adoration. Every breath and movement of hers was pure worship. See what praise Mary rendered her Son. This glorious bride of the Spirit accepted all of the joys and sorrows that were sent to her from that first day on, as so many tokens of love from her Beloved. Could anything break a relationship so closely bound to God? He was the living Fruit of Mary. She became the fruitful tree of Life which was described in the Old Testament. "Come to me, all you that yearn for me and be filled with my fruits, you will remember me as sweeter than honey." (*Sirach* 24:18,19 NAB). Mary wants us to seek her and receive her so that she can give us her Fruit, which is Jesus. "Resplendent and unfading is Wisdom, and she is readily perceived by those who love her and found by those who seek her." (*Wis.* 6:12 NAB).

All these things were given to me because I loved the Word of God. "Desire therefore my words; long for them and you shall be instructed." (*Wis.* 6:11 NAB). Praise God for His goodness! This was but the beginning of a profound understanding of His mysteries. Seek Wisdom, for "Wisdom leads up to a kingdom." (*Wis.* 6:20 NAB). Those who accept this teaching will also become as fruitful trees bearing the spiritual fruit of Christ, for "On either side of the river grew the trees of Life." (*Rev.* 22:2 NAB). Although Mary's fruit was the Messiah and the Word enfleshed in the body of Christ, the believer's fruit will be mostly hidden and spiritual until the Day of the Lord. Those whose hearts are pure will be able to discern that these things are of God. However, for some, this teaching will be difficult to understand, let alone accept. Let those who can, do. Simply have faith by believing that His Word is true and watch as He brings it to fulfillment.

Prompted by the Spirit and the advice of a priest, I wrote a letter explaining this vision to Pope Paul VI. To my surprise, I received an answer, together with a small gift. Because of this blessing and the response from Pope Paul, I knew that the Lord approved and this was His will. Jesus had told us that "None of those who cry out, 'Lord, Lord,' will enter the kingdom of God but only the one who does the will of my Father in heaven." (*Matt.* 7:21 NAB). It is important that we proceed to do His will as soon as we discover what it is so that His plan, not ours, is accomplished.

I did not have spiritual understanding until I surrendered my life in total consecration to Jesus through Mary. By living that consecration I began to have a new depth of understanding. Mary does indeed communicate and teach us about the mysteries of God just as Scripture relates: "Send her forth from your holy heavens . . . that she may be with me and work with me that I may know what is your pleasure." (*Wis.* 9:10 NAB).

Many people have asked for an explanation of Mary's presence at Pentecost, for some do not believe she was present in the Upper Room. Let us once again refer to the Word to find the truth. "And when they reached the city they went to the upper room . . . . All these joined in continuous prayer, together with several women, including Mary the mother of Jesus, and with his brothers." (*Acts* 1:13,14 TJB). Men and women were gathered together as the family of God on the occasion of the Pentecostal outpouring.

As they prayed for the promised Holy Spirit, they naturally centered their activity around the Bride of the Spirit, Mary. She was the only person in that room who had been previously overshadowed by the Holy Ghost. (*Lk.* 1:35). They were now her spiritual children. As she taught them to pray to the Spirit, they received the spiritual rebirth in the Spirit, which transformed them into adopted sons and daughters of God. "Those whom he foreknew he predestined to share the image of his Son, that the Son might be the first-born of many brothers." (*Rom.* 8:29 NAB). "He likewise predestined us through Jesus Christ to be his adopted sons ... that all might praise the glorious favor that he has bestowed on us in his Beloved." (*Eph.* 1:5, 6 NAB).

Pentecost is the occasion upon which the disciples were spiritually reborn through the power and presence of the Holy Spirit. "And of Zion they shall say: 'One and all were born in her: And he who has established her is the most High Lord.'" (*Ps.* 87:5 NAB). Each day they grew more in the image of God, and they rejoiced; for they knew "they are a chosen race, a royal priesthood, a holy nation ... who could show forth the praises of him who called them out of darkness into his marvelous light." (*1 Ptr.* 2:9 NAB).

I urge you to make a total consecration to Jesus through Mary. I know that great blessings have been received in my life because I have done this. "Those who serve her serve the Holy One; those who love her the Lord loves." (*Sirach* 4:14 NAB). As an example of these blessings, whenever I meditated upon some aspect of the Lord's life, I would somehow sense her presence interiorly. I knew she was teaching me and sharing certain mysteries with me, for "she knows and understands all things, and will guide me discreetly in my affairs." (*Wis.* 9:11 NAB).

Meditating upon the Stations of the Cross was one of my favorite devotions of my deep gratitude for all Jesus had done for me. One day, while I was lost in thought about His Crucifixion, I suddenly found myself in spiritual union with Mary. The Lord was dying, and I clung fiercely to His pierced feet. No power on earth could have loosened the steel grip of my arms which encircled the Savior's torn feet as I knelt there, dissolved in grief. She wept bitterly as she knelt at her Son's torn feet. There was no one to console her. The sword of grief had pierced her pure heart. They then took Him down from the Cross, and once more I felt this union as they gently lifted the crucified Christ into my arms for a last glance at Him. My heart was broken as I gazed upon His lifeless body and the gaping red holes in His wrists. I could not stop crying. His tortured body had been torn to shreds by iron hooks when He was so cruelly scourged. I knew the sentiments of our sorrowful Mother as I participated in her sufferings. Oh, what heart-rending grief was Mary's! The prophets foretold the martyrdom she went through when they wrote, "Come all you who pass by the way, look and see whether there is any suffering like my suffering." (*Lam.* 1:12 NAB).

The vision of that tragic day is as fresh in my mind now, after all these years, as it was the day it happened. The recollection still brings tears to my eyes. What can we do for all that Jesus and Mary suffered? What does His Word teach us? "Daughters of Jerusalem, do not weep for me. Weep for yourselves and for your children." (*Lk.* 23:28 NAB).

Do you see how Mary longs to instruct us about her Son? Like the prophet, let us ask the Father to "send her forth from you holy heavens and from your glorious throne dispatch her." (*Wis.* 9:10 NAB). Mary will wait for your invitation and will reveal her presence to you in one way or another, for "she hastens to make herself known in anticipation of men's desire." (*Wis.* 6:13 NAB).

Prepare yourself for her "because she makes her rounds seeking those who are worthy of her and graciously appears to them in the ways." (*Wis.* 6:16 NAB). She will lead you into a deep relationship with Jesus and the Holy Spirit. They will bring you closer to the Father. Do not say, "I have no need of Mary." The Trinity chose her above all others to fulfill Their design. You could make no better decision than to follow Their example. To reject Mary is to reject the Divine Purpose.

Let me tell you more about this highly favored daughter. On the anniversary of my father's death, I was at church praying just before receiving Communion. I asked Mary to give Jesus her love in place of mine because I felt so inadequate. My love is terribly shallow compared to hers. After coming back from Communion, I felt great peace in my heart. Suddenly Mary appeared close by (that is, in an interior vision). She seemed to be waiting for someone. Oh, how exquisite she looked as her long hair hung loosely beneath a golden veil. Her dress was also made of the same gold-colored material. She was radiant with glory. Later I discovered this verse: "The queen stood on thy right hand in gold of Ophir!" (*Ps.* 45:10 NAB) and "All glorious is the king's daughter as she enters; her raiment is threaded with spun gold." (*Ps.* 45:14 NAB). Then Jesus appeared beside her. He wore a white robe with a red tunic. They conversed for a few moments, but I was not permitted to hear them. I simply looked on. They then turned to me and He said to His Mother, "Look how she loves us."

My greatest desire then was to kiss the five most precious Wounds of Jesus, which to me are so many seals of honor now. I longed to show Him some sign of gratitude. Turning to Mary, I asked, "Please Mother, would you kiss the wounds of Jesus for me?" and she did. She also kissed His brow where the Crown of Thorns had been. Mary demonstrated the greatest degree of love possible for a creature to extend to the Most High. No one is capable of loving Jesus to the degree she has, for no one has ever had or will have the special unity she has enjoyed with God's Spirit. Then everything vanished, leaving my heart filled with joy.

I really did not expect anything like this to happen when I asked Mary to love Jesus for me. It was all so unexpected, but then Mary was so good. There is no question of evil interference in this experience because this was wholly interior, occurred at Communion time, and was a degree of mystic union with God.

In the period of the Later Church, there seem to be fewer manifestations of the Spirit. In the eighteenth century St. DeMontfort spoke prophetically about the Last Days, in which a spirit-filled people would bring about a great renewal upon the face of the earth. We are now in the beginning of that renewal. The Lord has poured out His Spirit as never before in history. His prophecy is being fulfilled in this day in those servants who have received the outpouring of the Spirit. Let me share with you a description of these servants of the Lord by St. Louis DeMontfort:

"They shall be ministers of the Lord who like burning fire, shall kindle the fire of divine love everywhere.

"They shall be the true apostles of the later times, to whom the Lord of Hosts shall give the word and the might to work marvels.

"They shall have in their mouths the two-edged sword of the Word of God.

"...They shall have the silvered wings of the dove, to go, with the pure intention of the glory of God and the salvation of souls, wheresoever the Holy Ghost shall call them.

"But who shall those servants, slaves, and children of Mary be? These are the great men who are to come..."[10]

In the Book of Hebrews we find similar statements about the days of the Messianic Enthronement, for St. Paul tells us, "He makes his angels winds, and his ministers flaming fire" (*Heb.* 1:7 NAB) and "Are they not all ministering spirits, sent to serve those who are to inherit salvation?" (*Heb.* 1:14 NAB). I see all these things taking place in our day. What an exciting time it is!

I have shared some of these experiences and teachings with clergymen and leaders of prayer groups within the country. They in turn have dedicated themselves and have written to tell me what happened. One pastor on the East Coast gave this teaching to those under his pastoral care, and hundreds of people received the outpouring of the Holy Spirit, committing themselves to the Lord through Mary. In a Pennsylvania town, half of the members of a seminary made this consecration and they, too, received the experience of Pentecost. It was in God's plan that a large group of representatives of all the religious orders in that area were to be at that seminary for the weekend for a retreat, and they too received the release of the Spirit. These are just a few of the many blessings which have taken place through the activity of the Holy Spirit and Mary.

When Mary accepted the word from God, she brought forth the Word in flesh through the Spirit. "In the beginning was the Word; the Word was in God's presence, and the Word was God." (*Jn.* 1:1 NAB). When we accept the word that God speaks in our hearts, when we accept Mary and the Holy Spirit, we too will bring forth Christ in our hearts in a supernatural way. Mary will help bring forth Christ in you, for this is part of her role as Mother of Christ's Mystical Body.

Mary was the vessel chosen to usher in the coming of Christ. "The salvation of the world began with the salutation of Mary," said Blessed Alan de La Roche.[11] She will also have a role in ushering in the second coming of Christ. We have only to look in the Book of Revelation to see her described as "A great sign . . . in the sky, a woman clothed with the sun, with the moon under her feet and on her head a crown of twelve stars." (*Rev.* 12:1 NAB). She is ready to give birth to a Child who would rule the earth. This Child can be identified as the members of the Body of Christ. We can also use the words of St. Paul to describe Mary: "You are my children, and you put me back in labor pains until Christ is formed in you." (*Gal.* 4:20 NAB). In *Revelations*, Satan wants to devour this Child, but Mary is caught up to God with the Child in her arms. This sounds to me like the rapture that is to come. "Then we, the living, the survivors, will be caught up with them in the clouds to meet the Lord in the air." (*1 Thess.* 4:17 NAB). As a people of God, we must intercede for all the brethren so that darkness may not overtake them. The Spirit and the Bride beckon us to "Come!" Let us imitate the Woman and respond by saying, "Let it be done!"

The Sword of the Spirit

–5–

Ecstatic Prayer

"Your old men shall dream dreams, your young
men shall see visions." (*Joel* 3:1 NAB)

When I was young, I had no regard for dreams, as we had been
taught they were nonsense. But I have discovered that in addition
to ordinary dreaming, there are supernatural dreams and prophetic
visions. Ordinary dreams are easily forgotten because they impart
no enlightenment, nor do they communicate any knowledge; however, divine dreams, like all true visions, are never erased from the
memory. In these dreams or visions, God speaks to us by giving us
a teaching, a consolation, a revelation, or a pre-vision of an event
which will happen in the future.

Once I understood this, I could see a striking similarity between the ecstatic vision, which occurs during waking hours, and
the divine dream. During both the divine dream and the ecstatic
vision, the Lord suspends the senses and then impresses upon the
spirit that which He desires to communicate to an individual. A
person in slumber can yet be united to God in a supernatural way
in exactly the same manner as one who is experiencing the ecstatic
vision. In either case, the senses of the individual are suspended so
that he may be receptive to infused contemplation. "He speaks by
dreams and visions that come in the night." (*Job* 33:15 TJB).

A dream which contains a word of wisdom (knowledge of the
future), a word of knowledge (a revelation of the past or of the

present), a discernment of spirits, or some other opening of the spiritual mysteries carries the signature of God and can be accepted. This is a function of the revelational gifts. This same principal applies to visions, since the two are almost identical.

The Lord has often communicated His will to man in these ways. An example of this is when the angel of the Lord appeared in a dream to Joseph and told him to take Mary and the Child to Egypt because Herod wanted to kill Jesus (*Matt.* 2:13, 14). Can you imagine what might have happened if Joseph had believed that dreams had no special meaning? But because Joseph was a man of God, he knew the ways of the Lord and promptly obeyed by fleeing into Egypt.

I believe that Joseph had the prophetic gift. God made known to prophets like Joseph and Daniel the mysteries of the future through the vehicle of supernatural dreams and visions. Man has no access to such information except through divine revelation. Of course, in those days there were no books to explain the various stages of contemplative prayer, so many of the visions that were recorded by the Scripture writers as dreams were in fact ecstatic prayers in mystical union with God. St. Jerome, we are told, made no distinction at all between the vision and the dream.

St. Jerome's studies also gave him good reason to value dreams and visions. In commenting on *Jeremiah* 23:25 ff., he shared Jeremiah's concern, indicating that dreaming is a kind of prophesying that God can use as one vehicle of revelation to a soul. It can be a valuable revelation from God if a man's life is turned toward him.[1]

In the Book of Daniel, the prophet is often called upon to interpret the king's dream, and he does so by using the revelational gifts which God had bestowed upon him. Daniel speaks to the king in these words: "These, then, are the dreams and the visions that passed through your head..." (*Dan.* 2:28 TJB). Here we have proof that Daniel knew that dream-visions were a sign from God and were not nonsense.

In the New Testament, we find that the Lord spoke to Peter, to Paul, to Annias, to John, and to others through dreams and visions. St. Chrysostom comments: "To some the grace was imparted through dreams, to others it was openly poured forth. For indeed by dreams the prophets saw, and received revelations."[2]

The Scripture urges us to "Let the prophet who has a dream recount his dream; let him who has my word speak my word truthfully!" (*Ger.* 23:28 NAB). Even today the Lord makes known His will through these same vehicles, but because of ignorance and wrong instruction, people do not comprehend their import.

Although I have had various experiences of these supernatural dreams and visions, I could not understand them; and especially when I was very young, I had no one to guide me. I feel that I have lost a great deal because of this, for I truly wish to know the Lord. Many times I have seen events take place in the spiritual realm years before they would happen. During ecstatic prayer I would see places and events which I had no knowledge of. When I would encounter these things later, I would think, "Haven't I been here before?" Unaccountably, everything would be exactly the same as that which was seen previously in the spiritual state. I now realize that this was the operation of the revelational gifts.

These dreams and visions began for me when I was only five or six years old. Children readily experience such things because their hearts are pure. We see accounts in the Bible where God spoke in this manner to children. For example, one night God called Samuel while he was sleeping, but Samuel did not recognize the voice of the Lord. He thought that Eli had called him. This happened several times before Samuel received a vision of God (*1 Sam.* 3:3-5). When Samuel awoke, he feared to tell Eli about the vision. But the Lord continued to speak to Samuel in this manner, and soon all of Israel knew that this young man "was an accredited prophet." (*1 Sam.* 3:20 NAB).

The prophets were the mouthpieces of the Lord. They were to preach and teach what God had given them in internal inspirations, visions, dreams, and signs. They were of all ages and both sexes. In the case of the latter, we have the teachings of both St. Thomas Aquinas and St. Benedict XIV:

From the theological point of view, St. Thomas arrived at the same solution: "The grace of prophecy is manifested according to the spirit illumined by God; and from this point of view there exists no difference between the sexes." (*Sum. Theol.*, II, 2, ad2).

And Benedict XIV approves the opinion of Mattheuccius; "One must not reject apparitions and visions because they have been perceived by women." From the point of view of the soul and spirit (Pneuma) there is no difference of sex. The suprasensible forces are not necessarily conditioned by the influence of sex.[3]

Women often filled prophetic roles in Biblical times. For example, "there was also a certain prophetess, Anna..." (*Lk.* 2:36 NAB). Elizabeth knew through internal inspiration that Mary was the Mother of the Lord, and prophesied it. Mary, in turn, prophesied when she proclaimed that one day all nations would call her blessed. The Book of Judges identifies yet another prophetess who served as a Judge of Israel. Whenever the Israelites wanted to know the will of the Lord, they would go to Deborah. She told them when to go into battle and how the enemy would be defeated. All of this was possible because she had the revelational gifts.

Although we have the testimony of Scripture and the teachings of the Doctors of the Church to rely on, it is sad to see the role of women in the Church limited because of ignorance or prejudice. When it comes to the operation of the Holy Spirit, can there be any such difference? Can this injustice stand before God? Interiorly, we are all made in the image of God. In affairs of the Spirit, it is the inner being that counts; the flesh means nothing.

Who is man to tell God that His Spirit cannot operate or move where He will? The Spirit of the Lord often used women in dramatic ways. As previously noted the Biblical prophetess Deborah told the army when to march and even walked with them. We see how women of the Covenant, such as Esther and Judith, were called upon to save the nation of Israel. The holy women of the New Testament did not abandon the Lord in His hour, but watched over Him at the Cross. Have we not proof enough that God can and will continue to speak through women as well as men? The Covenant women of today must follow this example: they too can help to build the Holy Nation, speak His Word, cling to His Cross, for indeed He has told us to do so. Let us not grieve the Spirit of God by actions which would stifle His work.

Both when I was a child and an adult, the Lord spoke to me through divine visions and dreams. Thus, He taught me His supernatural Word.

One man learns ... while awake, another while asleep. But in the waking state man is the teacher, whereas it is God who makes the dreamer fruitful with his own courage, so that learning and attaining are one and the same. Now to make fruitful is even more than to teach.[4]

It was in this manner, for example, that I was instructed to use Jesus' name in spiritual warfare. In a dream-vision, the Lord opened up to me the power to discern spirits, both good and evil. In the vision which opened this door for me, I saw with the spiritual sight of the intellect, four hideous, dwarf-like creatures approach me. They clamped their claw-like fingernails deep into the flesh of my arms. Although these fiendish creatures did not seem powerful, I could not dislodge them. I did everything I could think of to destroy them, but they would just dissipate and then re-integrate themselves again. This happened several times, and I became panic-stricken, for I did not know what to do.

In this night-time vision, I saw them huddled together underneath the pear tree in our yard, when I heard them say, "What can we do to her now?" In a united front, they assailed me again with those claws stabbing into my arms. By this time I was petrified because I was ignorant of spiritual warfare. In desperation I cried out, "Jesus, help me!" and immediately they let go of my arms and disappeared.

That night the Lord taught me the power of His holy name and its use in spiritual battle. In fact, it should be the battle cry of the victorious! For in no other way will you be able to conquer the spiritual enemy. Every knee, even the diabolical, has to bow down at the sound of this powerful name: Jesus. Use it to conquer in every situation. Satan fears this name, for by it he was defeated. He must bow at its utterance, and how can he fight you when he is on his knees? Thus the verse, "Use my name to expel demons" (*Mk.* 16:17 NAB) became a reality for me.

At still another time the Lord taught me more about the discernment of spirits. In a supernatural dream-vision, I saw before me a very polished man, and I thought he was of God. Everything about him seemed perfect, yet I sensed that he was evil, and deep dread came over me. Although he had a friendly smile, I was inspired to call out, "Jesus is my Lord" over and over. This was long before the phrase was used by Charismatics. As I repeated this, I watched this counterfeit angel of light change; his smile turned to an ugly scowl and his anger mounted. He was defeated through the name of the Lord and vanished quickly.

Do you see how the Lord was teaching in these instances? The Apostle John cautioned the children of God to test the spirits (*I Jn.* 4:1): If we listen to his warning, we will never be deceived. In my first dream-vision, the Lord opened my spiritual sight to see the evil spirits: they were not in disguise. In the second event, though the evil spirit came as a counterfeit angel of light, the internal inspiration helped me to discern who he was. The Lord was teaching me that we can appropriate all that He has given us in power and authority over evil. The two visions corroborate His promise: "I have given you power to tread on snakes and scorpions and all the forces of the enemy" (*Lk.* 10:19 NAB). If He has said it, you can do it! For those who desire to learn more concerning the gift of discernment of spirits, I would recommend St. Ignatious of Loyola's book, *The Spiritual Exercise.*

The Lord often uses supernatural dream-visions as a vehicle to teach, to console, to foretell events, and to warn people about dangers. After doing some research in this area, I found that others had experienced similar occurrences.

St. Alphonsus Liguori truly remarks that "the revelations of secret or of future things, such as the mysteries of the Faith, the reading of consciences, the predestination of certain persons, their death, their elevation to some dignity, and other similar things may occur in three ways: by visions, by locutions, and by a simple apprehending of the truth." (*Homo. apost.*, Appendix I, No. 22).[5]

The following prophetic vision was a revelation of the future, insofar as within ten days it all had come to pass. In this vision of the night I found myself standing in an unknown place somewhere on the crest of a hill. It was a beautiful countryside covered with green meadows and rolling hills scattered over with foliage and brush. In spite of the fact that I did not see any vehicles, I had a certain feeling that an automobile accident had taken place. As I stood on the hill crest, I looked towards the downward slope and saw the body of a young man with tousled hair lying in the brush. His identity was hidden from me, as his face was turned towards the ground. This was quite disturbing at first for I knew this young man had died. Suddenly, this scene vanished. I awoke momentarily because I was shaken. Then the Lord brought me back into that ecstatic prayer and I saw with the spiritual sight a large hand reach out to me with the Sacred Host held in the palm. I understood that I was to receive this Host as Communion. This mystical Communion brought me a great consolation.

Only ten days later, we received news that someone very close had just been in an auto accident in a locality similar to that which I saw in the divine dream. The young man involved had died. The only comfort I received at the funeral was that this person had accepted Jesus as Lord of his life several years previous. The mystical Communion which followed the accident in my vision, I believe, was an indication to me that the Lord was going to bring some good out of this apparent tragedy. I also accept it as a sign of the authenticity of the prophecy.

If things of which certain knowledge can only reach man by the will and grant of God, become known to man through a dream, they are of such kinds as are called "future contingencies" in the schools of theologians.[6]

Had I been more thoroughly grounded in the prophetic nature of dream, I would not have dismissed this warning quite so lightly. And I shall never do so again, for I have learned that if the matter of these prophetic dream-visions do come to pass, they must come from the Lord. Surely God does all that He can to get our attention so that we heed Him when He tries to communicate to us, but because of our ignorance we too often neglect to receive His word. St. Ambrose advises on this point: "Our God gives warnings in many ways, by heavenly signs, by the precepts of the prophets; by the visions even of sinners He wills that we should understand that we should entreat Him to take away all disturbances..."[7]

There is, as yet, so much to learn in this area; let us pray that the Holy Spirit will teach us to advance in the knowledge of His ways. Let us open our minds and our hearts to Him and be responsive to all that He gives in inspiration, and anointing.

I recall another time when the Spirit gave me another experience in vision concerning mystical Communion. Again I saw large hands, holding before me a large consecrated Host and a chalice filled with smaller hosts. I greatly desired to receive the large Host, but the hand put It aside and gave me the small Hosts, one by one, until I had consumed them all. This ecstatic prayer continued for hours until the morning came, and my heart was overflowing with joyful thanksgiving and peace.

I had made a habit of asking the Lord to release my spirit before going to sleep so that I might pray even while my body slept. I so longed to adore Him and praise Him that I thought of sleep as wasted time, so through inspiration this is what I asked of Him. Even though I slept, my spirit was keenly aware of the visitation of the Lord.

Like the maiden in the Song of Solomon (*Sg. of Sg.* 5:2) who tells that she sleeps, but her heart was awake — certainly in the night season the psalmist found that something came through to him which he knew as the revelation of God.[8]

The words of Isaiah are appropriate to describe my experience of that night: "You shall be visited by the Lord of hosts ... like a dream, a vision in the night." (*Is.* 29:6,7 NAB).

St. Ambrose comments upon the visitation of the Spirit in sleep.

"In his more theological writings Ambrose supported the idea that the Holy Spirit speaks through dreams. He showed that an angel who speaks through a dream is functioning at the direction of the Holy Spirit, since angelic powers are subject to and move by the spirit."[9]

Likewise, in *Psalm* 127:2 David notes the spiritual blessings the soul may receive as the body sleeps.

The dream is likened to the wish which has been fulfilled, and the poet goes on to strengthen this by showing that the Lord "gives to his beloved in sleep" what cannot be had simply by rising early and working late.[10]

Although I had never specifically asked to know the divine mysteries, I did have a great desire to understand more about such events as the Resurrection, the Ascension, and the Crucifixion. Because He knows our innermost thoughts and desires, He often fulfills them without our asking.

At this point I am reminded of a prayer of St. Alphonsus Rodriguez: "Lord, let me know Thee, and let me know myself." And, at once, he was lifted up above all created things. He found himself as it were in another region, alone with God, who gave him great light concerning the knowledge of God and of self...[11]

One evening, just before falling asleep, I began to contemplate the Resurrection and, as I did so, this vision came to me. Once more I found myself in an unfamiliar place, and I was climbing over large boulders up the side of a steep mountain. As I neared the summit, I heard a rumbling sound, as if a landslide were taking place. A huge boulder had worked itself loose and rolled down the mountain. Behind it was left an enormous cavity. I curiously edged my way over to the wide opening. It was the entrance to a long, dark tunnel. I entered, though I did not know where it led, and suddenly found myself in another cave-like room. I wondered where I was and sensed a presence behind me. I turned around and was so shocked that I almost fainted. There before my eyes was the dead body of the Christ lying on a rectangular slab of stone. Although it was very dark, I was very certain. I was grief-stricken as I beheld my Lord. I stood very close to Him as I observed His face, when suddenly His eyes opened and He looked directly into mine and smiled. I was so stunned that I fell back, in much the same way that the chief priests and Pharisees must have reacted when He revealed Himself by saying, "I am he" the night of His arrest in the garden of Gethsemane (*Jn.* 18:5 TJB). When I had sufficiently gained my composure, I noticed that He was now sitting up, then standing up only a short distance from me, a victorious expression on His face. Powerful vibrations of resurrected life filled the close space. Again, I heard a loud, rumbling noise. The mountain began to crumble, beginning at the peak. Simultaneously with the leveling of the mountain, I saw the Lord grow larger than normal in size, to even epic proportions, so that He covered the face of the earth. I was as a grain of sand at His feet; yet, I had no fear, as His face radiated love.

Even though I felt I had a greater understanding of the Resurrection as a result of this vision, many times the Lord does not immediately impart the complete meaning of any one vision. This is typical of the words He speaks through visions and dreams. Now, it is my belief that during Christ's entombment, Mary was spiritually transported into the tomb to be with her Son. I believe that Mary was teaching me about the event of His Resurrection and that somehow the mountain in the vision is symbolic of the Mother of Christ. Let me explain.

Zechariah, the prophet, proclaimed that in the Messianic days the Lord would return to the holy city Jerusalem and to Zion, the holy mountain (*Zc.* 8:2-4). And in the very next chapter, he refers to Zion and Jerusalem as "daughter" (*Zc.* 9:9 NAB).

Who shall ascend into the mountain of the Lord? asks the Prophet; that is to say, who shall come to a perfect union with her whom the Holy Ghost called the mountain of God where Jesus always dwells and teaches the meaning of the eight beatitudes; and the Prophet answers, "The innocent in hand and the clean of heart. Never will you draw her into your soul where she wishes to rule as Queen, unless you abhor sin and have a great desire to become perfect."[12]

Don't you agree that this sounds like a description of Mary, the queen who abhors sin, the model of the beatitudes, the instructress of perfect union with the Holy Spirit? If we can see Mary as the "holy mountain," then we can see that on the Last Day Christ will emerge triumphant from time's womb and transcend it, just as on the Nativity He was born of Mary's womb with the purpose of transcending the flesh and overcoming the death all flesh is heir to. Now do you see that within the word of knowledge given me about the Resurrection was also a word of prophecy, less readily apparent, about the role of Mary in the Final Days?

As we have seen, St. Jerome had great faith in the capacity of divine dreams to impart knowledge of a very privileged kind. We are told he believed "dreaming is a kind of prophesying that God can use as one vehicle of revelation to a soul. It can be a valuable revelation from God if a man's life is turned toward Him.[13] But in addition to imparting knowledge and conveying prophecies, the divine dream can be the occasion of even more amazing spiritual gifts. "We are told that, as in the case of St. Paul and other prophets, what begins as a divine dream will be converted by God into an ecstatic or rapturous experience."[14] In this type of experience, everything occurs in an eternal now — time as we know it ceases to be and the past, present, and future are eternally one.

Ezekiel 8:2 shows that "the visions make as if possible to know the sacred things," while the next verse reveals that the prophet, because he was carried there "not in body, but in the spirit." Thus the dream-vision is seen as transcending time and space.[15]

The supernatural dream, or dream-vision, is often a combination of the mystical union with God in obscurity or darkness, which is known in contemplative writings as "the ray of divine darkness." The spirit of a person is caught up into this obscurity of God, who brings the human spirit where He desires and teaches it what He deems is most beneficial for it or for the good of others. I call this an obscurity because it surpasses anything our intellects can explain, and so it remains thus until we see Him face-to-face.

In the Spiritual Canticle, on the contrary, [he] says clearly that the transformation is only reached by the way of ecstasy; "The spiritual flight signifies a certain high estate and union of love, whereunto, after many spiritual exercises, God is wont to elevate the soul; it is called the Spiritual Espousals of the Word ... The first time that God so elevates the soul, He reveals to it great things of Himself." (*A Spiritual Canticle*, Stanza XIV, p. 74).[16]

In a rapture experience the spirit travels at an enormous rate of speed which exceeds anything we know on earth. The spirit which is caught up in the Lord or by His Spirit in rapture can be halfway around the earth in just a few seconds. It seems to me that because they are called "children of light" in Scripture, the faithful are somehow able to move in the Spirit as fast as light. This is the only comparison I can think of to illustrate the phenomenon. We have the teaching of St. Alphonsus Liguori to inform us about the flight of the spirit:

> A person who has received this grace told me that in these elevations of the spirit, it seemed to her that her soul was torn from the body and violently lifted up as though she traversed in an instant a thousand miles. And this was a great terror to her, for she did not know whither she was going. When she stopped, she was enlightened by some divine secret.[17]

There were times when I experienced these supernatural states during night vigils of the spirit, for "I was sleeping, but my heart kept vigil." (*Sg. of Sg.* 5:2 NAB). "My soul yearns for you in the night, yes, my spirit within me keeps vigil for you." (*Is.* 26:9 NAB).

There were even times when I awoke because my spirit was praising God so loudly and I rejoiced.

The Jesuit "director of mystics" Scaramelli has described these states:

> This is a special kind of ecstasy. He calls it spiritual sleep, taking this word in a sense that is not St. Teresa's. He supposes, at least, that such a state leaves good effects behind it; the soul comes to herself again in a profound peace; the mind remains attached to God and detached from creatures. It is solely because of these effects that he judges the state to have been supernatural.[18]

We understand now how it is possible to praise God without ceasing and to fulfill this command of Christ. He who is all-powerful would not ask us to accomplish something that is beyond our power to do. His grace is available, even as we sleep, to those who ask for it. We have only to show ourselves responsive to all He desires to give us.

When St. Peter announced to the first gathering of Christians the realization of the prophecy of Joel: "I will pour out my Spirit upon all flesh: and your sons and your daughters shall prophesy..." he was applying this to the whole Church — to men and women in all walks of life, old people and young people. He certainly intended to say that in the Messianic epoch the Spirit of God could manifest Itself in any member of the Church; no one was excluded in advance from the gift of prophecy or of visions.[19]

Now this type of ecstatic prayer can and does take place during the day. It has the same effects as the dream-visions, for they are almost identical.

St. Teresa describes what takes place in a rapture in this way:

> The soul is asleep, fast asleep, as regards the world and itself ... being unable to think on any subject (save God) even if it would. The soul is deprived of the faculties it exercised while in the body.[20]

This violent motion cannot, as a rule, be resisted. These raptures are "very alarming, especially at first."[21]

I have found this to be true from my own experience. Once, while I was standing in line to receive the Sacrament of penance, I felt a dense heaviness come over me. I felt almost as if I would faint or collapse under the weighty feeling, which is called the ligature. There seemed to be a denseness all around me. Later I learned that this was the presence of the Lord as He was suspending the sense faculties. Somehow I managed to get into the confessional, and almost immediately I saw the vision of the face of Christ as He was hanging upon the Cross. This interior vision brought me to the deepest contrition I have ever known. It was to this suffering Christ that I confessed and repented of my sins. So absorbed was I in the Lord, who was before me, that I could barely hear the words of the priest.

Upon leaving the confessional, I again felt this overwhelming presence of the Lord. No sooner had I knelt to pray when suddenly I was caught up by the Spirit of the Lord in rapture. My spirit felt as if it had been torn from my body and taken away at rapid speed. I found myself standing in a crowd of people on a cobblestone street in the city of Jerusalem. It had been the same with the prophet Ezekiel, who wrote, "The spirit lifted me into the air and, in visions from God, took me to Jerusalem." (*Ezk.* 8:3 TJB).

As I looked around I noticed dwellings of stone and clay bleached by the sun. The people were wearing the style of clothing common in Biblical days, and I was as one of them. They seemed to be waiting for a procession of some kind to come down the street. They were angry, though, and their anger was directed toward a man who was slowly making his way toward us. He was carrying a crossbeam which weighed him down into a bent position. The skin on his face and arms was all bruised and bleeding. I wondered who the man was and why these people hated him so. In their anger, the people began to shout and jeer at him. They hit him and threw things. For some unknown reason I too threw a stick at him. Suddenly, he paused and looked right through me with the most compassionate and forgiving eyes. All at once my understanding was opened and I realized who He was. In that one majestic glance towards me, He revealed Himself. He said nothing; He didn't have to. This was the Christ, the Son of God! What had I done? My heart and spirit were crushed, and I sank into a well of sorrow such as I never thought possible. My eyes burned with tears. Now this kind of sorrow cannot be born of flesh, for it is an undeserved grace from the merciful hand of God. This Majesty of Love was not angry with me; He could only forgive those who had hurt Him. And that was the supreme moment of forgiveness.

Let me support the previous paragraph with the teaching of the scholar Augustine Poulain, who has this to say about ecstatic prayer.

"At the time we are enlightened as to our unworthiness, the contrast will be so striking that we shall feel a sentiment of self-disgust and horror."[22]

Surely this was true in what I felt after that penetrating glance of the Savior. But then I suddenly found myself back in the church, the "Our Father" still upon my lips. Such a sudden reunion of body and spirit is not unusual.

When the soul comes out of a rapture that has overtaken her in the middle of a conversation or prayer, it often happens that she continues the phrase where it was broken off.[23]

Almost immediately the intense sorrow I felt was changed into joyous exultation as I experienced an inpouring of the Spirit to such a degree that being could not contain that which was given. The skin on my body felt as if it would burst. I had never before or again experienced such happiness. I can understand now how the martyrs were able to endure their torments. The Lord supported them with this great joy. I began to sing praise to the Lord, and my heart was totally dedicated to the Lord from that moment on.

Lopez de Ezquerra, a priest-author and mystical teacher has this to say:

> All passive and extraordinary communications proceeding from a good spirit ... produce an efficacious excitation to good works ... and the soul feels that this movement come not from herself but from the divine virtue. She is conscious of an overflowing life...[24]

This was the day when I experienced that precious anointing of the Holy Spirit, the baptism of fire, which began to make me hunger for an even deeper relationship with Christ. He drew me with the strength of a steel magnet. This happened to me twenty years ago, yet it is as yesterday. It is something you can never forget, yet this is typical of mystical experiences for:

> The full plenitude of the understanding is retained during the rapture; it even seems to be enlarged and that there is a growth of activity in the higher faculties. All ecstatics affirm this fact, which stands out in all that they tell us concerning the mysteries that have been revealed to them.[25]

To hunger and thirst for the divine food of Christ is to open our spirits for communication with God, for "The hungry he has filled with good things." (*Lk.* 1:53 TJB). We grow in union with God through the reception of the Sacraments, which increase the God-life within us. Through the Eucharist, Christ re-creates us and transforms us into a reflection of the divine image as adopted children of God. Jesus has promised us, "Anyone who eats this bread will live forever." (*Jn.* 6:58 TJB).

Jesus has revealed Himself to me not only through the Sacrament of Penance, as I have described, but also in the Eucharist. One day at the Consecration of the Host during Mass, the Spirit prompted me to pray in this way: "Lord, are You in all Your glory today, or are You in the form of the Suffering Servant?" I could not understand why I said that, but the Spirit prays as He will through a person. Right after receiving Communion, while I was still kneeling at the altar rail, I had a vision of the Lord as the Suffering Servant. Once more I saw Him nailed to the Cross and in terrible agony. Blood streamed down His tortured arms from the nails in His wrists. It had happened so quickly that I was shocked as if by lightning. I really had not expected any response to my prayer, least of all this. Mentally I cried out, "Lord, take this away; I can't bear to see You like this!" Immediately it vanished. I deeply regret that I was unable to yield totally to what He was teaching me then.

Visions which take place within the context of the Sacraments are especially part of what is known as the mystical union and should not be regarded as mere illusions. Augustine Poulain, a master of the interior life, explains:

> Let's also note that the rejection of visions should not apply to those that are deific (Indeiques), those of the Divinity. For these are merely a kind of mystical union. It is a question of exdeific visions, those of created things. St. John of the Cross, although so rigid with regard to visions, notes this exception expressly: "This knowledge relates directly unto God, in the deepest sense of some of His attributes ... This becomes pure contemplation ... It is only a soul in union with God that is capable of this profound, loving knowledge, for it is itself that union ... It is God Himself who is felt and tasted...[26]

There are four rules for the spiritual director to follow in regard to revelations and visions. The fourth of these is: "to bear in mind the end to which visions, and especially revelations, tend ... This end may be solely to augment the love of God, Our Lord, the Blessed Virgin, and the saints in the seer of vision."[27]

The interior vision in which I saw Christ immediately after Communion so grounded me in faith in the true presence of Christ that I had no other choice but to run to Him each day to be nourished and strengthened. It has been twenty years since then, and He has filled me with the best of wheat.

Jesus, in the Eucharist, is the sign which brings us into the new covenant. By receiving this Sacrament, we are united to Christ as brothers and sisters. This Sacrament of His blood cleanses and strengthens us in our spiritual passage towards the great day of the Lord. We see this in the Book of Revelation: "These are the ones who have washed their robes and made them white in the blood of the Lamb." (*Rev.* 7:14 NAB).

As time passed, I experienced other types of unions, among which was one which is called an intellectual vision.

As the *experience* of bodily things is gained by the bodily senses, so too the *experience* of spiritual things gained in the superior part of the soul by spiritual senses.[28]

It was while I was reading about the Lord one day that I began to meditate and understand this teaching. As I glanced out of the window momentarily, I saw the Lord present in everything that existed. It was as if a veil had been removed from my understanding and sight as I saw things in a dimension beyond the natural world. Like an explorer discovering a new earth, I could see beyond the surface of all life, and my gaze penetrated into the invisible, interior core of all that was. The Lord was hidden within all these things, and I perceived Him in a new way. This perception of God can be described an immersion or envelopment of all life within a divine atmosphere.

St. Theresa of Avila, a Doctor of the Church, tells us:

> God is sometimes pleased, while a person is engaged in prayer, and in perfect possession of her senses, to suspend them and to discover sublime mysteries to her, which she appears to behold within God Himself ... This is no imaginary vision, but a highly intellectual one, wherein is manifested how all things are beheld in God, and how He contains them within Himself. It is of the greatest value, for although passing in an instant, it remains deeply engraved in the memory.[29]

Therefore, one could describe such an intellectual vision as a gaze into the spiritual realm by means of the gifts of wisdom and understanding. Through the five senses one can see, touch, taste, and feel the invisible presence of the Lord. In intellectual visions of the Divinity, God permits "the soul to lose herself in Him more or less deeply. But ordinarily, He did not allow Himself to be seen."[30] Such an experience becomes possible only when God lifts the veil from our eyes and permits us to see a greater dimension of life coexisting in the lives of all.

The Lord speaks in the mode of expression He chooses, and this may be followed by a flow of song or verse which tries to describe that which has been experienced. St. Teresa of Avila describes the difficulty of articulating these experiences:

> While the soul is in this ecstasy, our Lord favours
> it by discovering to it secrets such as heavenly
> mysteries and imaginary visions ... But when the
> visions are intellectual, *they are not thus easily
> related...*[31]

Though the weakness of our humanity cannot bear to see God as He is in the Beatific Vision, He does reveal Himself at various times in our individual lives. Though hidden, here and now He is part of us and we are part of Him; He is not far distant. When the breezes blow through, it is because His total Being is moved. He is thus present in the most insignificant ways — in the leaves and in the blades of grass. When He moves, all life moves in unison with Him. Now I can understand why holy people would not harm so much as the least of His creatures. Although He is always in our midst, we know it not.

To perceive God in this way is a very precious thing. Try as I may, I find it almost impossible to describe or to recapture. The verse which follows was recorded following the intellectual vision mentioned above.

Mystic Sight of the Incomprehensible

I looked through the veil at my God and saw
Him looking back at me in a multitude of
Varied expressions, radiantly beautiful!
I rested in loving thoughts about HIS LOVE
And saw Him in His world moving in rhythm.
He was the noble quality in each being:
He IS that noble quality of children —
Their transparent purity, their simplicity.
The rays of diaphanous light are but the
Shadows of His radiating LIGHT!
His Strength as firm as a giant sequoia tree,
The hurricane force but a whisper of His Power.
Are there words, my God, to tell Your people
Of Thee? How I long for them also to see!
His voice echoes sweetly in the twilight song

Of the modest thrush; the cricket gently betrays
His hidden presence and squeaks, "I'm here, I'M
   HERE."
The summer breeze enfolds us in His loving arms;
His fragrance enraptures one more
   than all the flowers combined.
He is ALL in all — a combination of earth's
   sweetest treasures; the purest honey,
   the look of the doe, her great grace —
   how intoxicating!
What pleasure to see Thy unknown form
within the forms of all, within the great and small!
He's ALL! He's ALL!

Many others have experienced the presence of God within the world of matter and nature in this way. One of these was Pierre Teilhard De Chardin. He also had a vision, which was very much like the one just described, of God's distinct yet complex presence in all of His creation. In his book *The Hymn of the Universe,* De Chardin tells us about his revelation:

> A being was taking form in the totality of space, a Being with the attractive power of a soul, palpable like a body, vast as the sky, a Being which mingled with things yet remained distinct from them; a Being of a higher order than the substance of things with which it was adorned, yet taking shape with them.
>
> I bless you, matter, and you I acclaim ... as you reveal yourself to me today in your totality and your true nature.[32]

P. Teilhard De Chardin — priest, scientist, mystic, and author — was a spirit-filled man endowed with a capability to understand supernatural truths in great depth. He must have been blessed with the charismatic gifts, for his writings give witness to the fact that he praised God in tongues and therein he speaks of being drawn into a spiritual fire. He surely experienced fifty years ago what those in the Charismatic Renewal are experiencing today, and this was no less than his own personal encounter with God's Spirit. De Chardin writes: "He would inevitably speak henceforth in an incomprehensible tongue, he whom the Lord had drawn to follow the road of fire."[33]

Through all of the experiences of the saintly men and women given above, together with the confirmation of Scripture itself, do you see that God even today is continually revealing Himself to His people? Surely He does speak to us with supernatural words, but we perceive it not. We should pray that He opens our spiritual faculties so that when He does speak, we will not fail to grasp His word.

The Benedictine Blosius warns us about heeding the worldly senses rather than the spiritual. "It grieves His divine Spirit to see us content with the lowest things, when He is ready to bestow on us the highest, for He desires to give Himself to us in the most excellent way."[34]

St. Ignatius expresses similar sentiments in a letter to St. Francis Borgia (Rome, 1548) when he writes, "All these very holy gifts should be preferred to all corporal acts of mortification."[35] And of course there is St. Paul's advice: "Set your hearts on spiritual gifts — above all, the gifts of prophecy." (*1* Cor. 14:1 NAB).

The gifts of contemplation, dream-visions, and ecstasy are all charismatic gifts of revelation which operate in the context of prophecy. Thus knowledge of the mysteries of God is transmitted interiorly as a result of mystic union with Him. The prophet Daniel knew of "things to come" because of the deep personal relationship he shared with God. "He reveals deep and hidden things and knows what is in the darkness, for the light dwells within him" (*Dan.* 2:22 NAB).

Mature Christians will have little trouble believing that the Holy Spirit is guiding His people, even through prophecy. Of course, the unbeliever will be skeptical. But "You are the heirs of the prophets, the heirs of the covenant God made with our ancestors" (*Acts* 3:25 TJB). Surely if the Lord spoke to our ancestors in this way, He will speak to us also. Yes, God does speak to those who love Him. Do not despise His word or His communications when they come, for they are the fulfillment of the prophecy of Joel that "Your sons and daughters shall prophesy, your old men shall dream dreams, your young men shall see visions." (*Jl.* 3:1 NAB).

–6–

The Radiance of Divine Glory

For many years I have pondered deeply upon the meaning of the glory of God which had often been mentioned in the homilies which I had heard. Was this celestial glory a tangible thing, or was it perceived only through the spiritual senses? Being inquisitive, I began to meditate upon Scripture to find the answer.

I learned that certain prophets were blessed by God with experiences of the Shakinah glory. I also learned that in later ages there were (certain) people who were very intimate with God and were favored with these experiences in which they caught a glimpse of His glory. The common feature of all these experiences was a deep interpersonal relationship with the Lord.

In Old Testament history, God made a covenant with Abraham, the twelve tribes of Israel, and their descendants. He told them, "I will be your God: and you will be my people." The Lord gathered these people, Israel, together as His family, and they looked to God as their Father. Yahweh gave His word that He would dwell with these people, and He was present to them under symbolic forms. For example, in the book of Exodus, the invisible God-Head presented Himself to His people in this way: "In the daytime the cloud of the Lord was seen over the Dwelling: whereas at night fire was seen in the cloud by the whole house of Israel in all the stages of their journey." (*Ex.* 40:38 NAB). This veiled presence of God was as a shield of protection for them.

When the Ark of the Covenant was built, the Lord was present as a radiating light, or a Cloud, hovering over the Ark, which was placed within the tent of meeting or the assembly place. This presence in the Holy of Holies was a guiding and sustaining force for the faithful of Yahweh. As the Covenant people gathered together to offer unto God the sacrifice of praise and thanksgiving, His glory was visibly apparent. "All the sons of Israel, seeing the fire come down and the glory of Yahweh resting on the Temple, bowed down..."(*2 Ch.* 7:3 TJB).

Many times this radiance was momentarily apparent over an assembly of persons who renewed the covenant between God and His people. This light of glory was often an indication that a certain people had been chosen for some special work by the Lord. For example, when Moses withdrew into the solitude of Mount Sinai to seek the Lord, he called out to God to reveal His presence: "Show me your glory." (*Ex.* 33:18 TJB). He waited prayerfully upon the Lord until He saw and heard the living Word appear to Him in a radiant glory of fire and light. His prayer was answered! Moses surrendered himself to this Presence in glory and received the Living Word and a portion of that glory into His own spirit. We can gain some understanding of this when we read, "He put his own light into their hearts to show them the magnificence of his words." (*Eccl.* 17:7 TJB). Now the Word and the Light were one and the Presence of God. When Moses received the Word and the Light of God into his spirit, he became empowered and enlightened by the means of contemplation and mystic union to accomplish his role in salvation history. When we look into the New Testament, we see that Jesus is known as the Light and the Word, for "The Word was the true light that enlightens all men." (*Jn.* 1:9 TJB). In the Old Testament, Moses experienced the Lord on Mount Sinai in the same way.

In the sacred silence of Sinai, Moses had emptied his heart before God and had thus fulfilled the necessary condition to receive the living Word into his own spirit,or heart. Blessed John Tauler often wrote about these attitudes so necessary for so great a blessing. He explains:

> Therefore, in proportion as thou dost earnestly
> gather inward all thy faculties in forgetfulness of

> all created things and of all their similitudes, be-
> ing recollected in thyself in obliviousness of crea-
> tures, the nearer art thou to receive the generation
> of the Divine Word.[1]

When Moses received this generation of the Word, he experienced a spiritual transformation. As the Fire diminished within the
burning bush, a portion of its transfiguring light entered into this
man of God and radiated from his countenance to such a degree
that the people were afraid. Moses now steps forward, empowered
by the Lord and endowed with all spiritual gifts necessary to fulfill
his mission. The confirmation of such an inter-relationship with
God is thus confirmed by supernatural wonders. The interior transformation that Moses and the disciples experienced were identical.
The outward signs differed slightly. Moses' face shone with light.
The disciples were crowned with tongues of fire. But St. Ambrose
teaches that God manifests His glory in both forms. "This surely is
the Holy Spirit who is called both fire and light of the Lord's countenance; the light as we have said, The light of Thy countenance, O
Lord is signed upon us."[2]

We see, then, the same Cause working through the Spirit to
bring forth a prophetic people who will witness to the indwelling
Presence of God by word and deed in order to bring about the
Kingdom of Heaven.

These findings satisfied my curiosity somewhat, but I wondered if there were any others throughout the ages who had also
experienced the glory of God. If so, who were they and what was
the effect of this perception of glory within their lives?

In my research, I came across the life story of another man
who greatly desired to know the Lord; his name was Francis of
Assisi. He also went up into the solitude of a rugged hilltop called
Mt. La Verna to seek God in prayer and detachment. As he heard
the Gospels of Christ, his inner being was overcome by the Spirit
of the Lord.

> Francis listened reverently. It was the Word of God.
> A great light came over him... Francis felt streams
> of light pouring over him. God had spoken.[3]

In this ecstatic state, Francis was enveloped within the light of glory and the fiery Presence of God which illuminated the whole of Mt. La Verna, so much so, that the entire mountain appeared to be burning. Meanwhile, Francis was burning with the fire of divine love. Here is a description of the event:

> Then the whole mount of La Verna seemed to flame forth with dazzling splendour, that shone and illuminated all the mountains and valleys round about, as if the sun were shining upon the earth. When the Shepherds that were watching in that country saw the mountain aflame and so much brightness about they were sore afraid ... The flame had endured over the mountain of La Verna for the space of an hour or more.[4]

When we compare the revelations of Moses and St. Francis, we see a striking similarity. Both men were seeking God in the prayerful seclusion of the summits and awaiting the Lord's response. His response came in a blaze of glory which radically changed them from ordinary people into spiritual giants. In both cases, Francis and Moses, descending from the summit, reflected the Shakinah glory they had seen, not only in beauty but in the power to do a work for the Lord. God repeatedly used this pattern of revelation and anointing in many instances when selecting a person for a mission. With these revelations of God, the selected person's will was brought into perfect alignment with the will of God.

A good example of this is the event of St. Paul's election: "There came a light from heaven all around him" (*Acts* 9:4 TJB). Paul was overcome by the radiant power of the Lord and was "slain in the Spirit" while the brightness of the Light of Christ blinded him. He later inquired as to who this Presence was and he heard these words: "I am Jesus." (*Acts* 9:5 TJB). Immediately he surrendered his will to the Lord in complete obedience and was ready to serve God. It was with this event that Paul was radically transformed from a persecutor of the brethren into a great missionary who would build up the Kingdom of God.

Undoubtedly the manifestations of the divine glory was one of God's ways of communicating to those whom He would use in a significant mission to His people. These divine commissions, which we have examined in the lives of Moses, St. Francis, and St. Paul, have been experienced by numerous other friends of God. For example, we have the writings of the mystic Marie Tessonier, who also saw this living light:

> What I saw was not a Light like that of the sun of the day, yet it shed a wonderful clarity, and from it proceeded all earthly and spiritual light. What I saw occupied no space, yet filled everything. It moved not, yet it animated and operated in all creation.[5]

This Light of God, which has manifested itself in history, is but a torch compared to what will one day appear throughout the celestial Jerusalem as "it was lit by the radiant glory of God." (*Rev.* 21:23 TJB). The fullness of God's glory, together with the glory of His people, will then be revealed. "When Christ, our life, appears, then we shall appear with Him in glory." (*Col.* 3:4 TJB).

This glorious Presence of Light is thoroughly imbued with supernatural power. When this penetrating power envelopes a person, it absorbs him into the Light. It then enlightens, transforms and recreates that person by degrees into its own glorious essence. It is not important what symbolic form God chooses to use to manifest Himself — fire, light, or a cloud. The important things for us to recognize is that He is truly present with power to transform His people into purified vessels capable of transmitting His power and glory. What is vital is that a person become totally surrendered to the Lord, ready to receive the dictates of the divine will so that God can use one as a vehicle of His love for the world.

The Light of God is not the name of a thing. It is to call forth an archetypal symbol of power and energy.[6]

Jesus often referred to the fact that He had power to cast out the darkness of evil and to bring forth new life through a transformation process.

Believers in the Twentieth Century are beginning to see these same manifestations of God's Spirit. When Christians gather together to pray and praise the Lord, this glory of God is oftentimes visible to them. Some of the people that we ministered to witnessed to the fact that their decisive point of commitment for the Lord took place when they perceived this Light during prayer. One person, whose heart was terribly hardened, immediately yielded to the Spirit upon seeing this Light and, falling upon his knees, asked that the Lord give to him the baptism of the Holy Spirit. At the same moment, when we began to pray with him, I saw and felt intense waves of power and light entering into him. His prayer was answered, as the Lord sent forth His power to transform him from "glory to glory into his image..." (*2 Cor.* 3:18 NAB).

At another time, a woman saw this Light during a witness talk, and the Lord touched her heart so that she immediately asked for prayer for the release of the Spirit of God. Previously, this same woman had had several miscarriages during pregnancy and desperately wanted a child. Again prayers were offered up, and within less than a year she was blessed with her first ten-pound baby boy. Her faith and commitment to Christ have grown tremendously since the time of that initial outpouring of the Spirit upon her.

The heart of Christ is filled with a burning love for His people. "I have come," He said, "to cast fire on the earth..." (*Lk.* 12:49, 50 NAB). He blesses His Body upon earth with the same baptism He received. As a People, we must be willing to receive His Presence — in Light, in Fire, in glory — in order to become the reflection of His image, in order to be a light to all nations. We must give all in total surrender in order to become sons of light.

Those who are seeking a deeper understanding of the risen Christ will find that the prayerful and meditative reading of Scripture will give many new insights to dwell upon. Jeremiah tells us, "Call to me, and I will answer you; I will tell you great mysteries of which you know nothing." (*Jr.* 33:3 TJB). When I acted upon these words, the Lord began to teach me that which I desired to know concerning His glory.

To continue with this theme, then, we see that Jesus permitted His disciples to see Him in a glorified state. "The Word was made flesh, he lived among us, and we saw his glory." (*Jn.* 1:14 TJB). When Jesus became incarnate, He divested Himself of His glory; that is, with the exception of the transfiguration at Mount Tabor. It was on the summit of Tabor that "His face shone like the sun and his clothes became as white as the light." (*Matt.* 17:2 TJB). Not only did the disciples witness the glory of the Son, but they experienced the overshadowing of a bright Cloud (*Matt.* 17:5-7) and heard the voice of the Father instructing them to listen to Jesus. Overcome with fear and their own preoccupation of building a tent, they did not grasp the significant words of Christ, who spoke of His "passing." Jesus was revealing His mission as the Savior who would glorify His Father by His impending Passion and death. This was His moment of glory! He pointed to it, but His disciples did not grasp it. And the Father glorified the Son at that moment! We also note in the Gospel of St. John that Jesus here spoke of His death as His hour of glory: "Now the hour has come for the Son of Man to be glorified." (*Jn.* 12:23 TJB). The disciples were brought to Tabor in order to be prepared and strengthened for Calvary. He told them to take up their cross as He would do.

If you will recall the account above, St. Francis was enveloped by the bright Fire of the Lord in much the same way that the Apostles were on Mount Tabor. Though the expression of these events may differ, in essence they are the same. Francis, as well as the Apostles, were to be living witnesses of the Suffering as well as the Risen Christ. In the brilliant presence of the Risen Lord himself, Francis was marked with the stigmata and was made a living image of the Crucified One.

Frequently we hear of those who were close to God experiencing His Presence in glory as a confirmation to do the work of the Lord by preaching, healing and prophesying. Of course, few have received the extraordinary grace of the stigmata, but all were called to suffer persecution for the cause of the Kingdom. No one can share in Christ's life except through participating in His suffering. All who are incorporated into Christ will, of necessity, have to undergo this transformation process to attain the perfection that the Father so desires of us. Christ told His disciples to be as perfect as His Father. And Jesus became the example of our perfection through His obedient suffering and death. As Jesus glorified the Father through His obedient suffering, so must His People glorify the Father through sharing the sufferings of the Son unto Resurrection. The Apostles, disciples and members of the early Church suffered and so, throughout the ages, all must share in the Cross of Christ for He, Himself, has said so.

In *Genesis* we read that God created man in His image; that is, man is like God in his spirit. Now then, Satan attempts to disfigure that spiritual image by replacing it with His demonic spirits, who tempt us to sin. When we consent to these temptations and sin, we permit his evil image to be reflected within us instead of the pure image of God. Christ came to restore that divine image within fallen man. When we repent of sin and yield to the purifying action of His Spirit, that restoration of mankind's original image takes place.

Today this same Spirit of God is being poured out upon the earth as never before. Thousands upon thousands are being renewed and restored to the divine pattern. I once saw this Taboric Transformation nearly completed within one of His people. This remarkable event took place during a retreat in which a guest celebrant had offered the Liturgy. During the Consecration and elevation of the Eucharist, the physical appearance of the priest was dramatically changed. His countenance and vestments were radiant with a light from within. I perceived the indwelling Presence of the risen Christ within the priest. I was stunned by the sight! But after a short while the priest's normal appearance was restored. This unexpected event was but another step in my understanding more about God's glory.

As time passed, the Lord taught me still more by giving me other personal glimpses of this glory. These experiences always took place within the context of the Sacraments, and were marked with a sense of mystical union. Once I somehow perceived a white light diffused within my being, but I could not explain this even to myself, nor could I comprehend at that time. How does one perceive light within the interior of one's own being? After years of searching, I found an explanation.

Thus the soul that is enclosed in the midst of God sees Him, and knows Him from all sides by the aid of that bright light that God communicates to her for the purpose of seeing and tasting Him.[7]

Alvarez de Paz, the Jesuit professor and Provincial of Peru, also write about this type of experience:

> In this supernatural manner the soul knows God
> in the depths of her being, and she sees Him, so to

say, more clearly than she sees the material light
with the eyes of the body. She sees God ... All takes
place in the summit of the spirit.[8]

And about this indwelling of the light, Scripture says: "The
Lord shall be your light." (*Is.* 60.19 NAB).

Jesus has said that if we keep His word — that is, the Com-
mandments and all His teachings — and if we love Him and accept
His Lordship over our lives, then He and His Father will indeed
come and abide with us and reveal His Presence to us. Scripture
confirms this in John: "I shall love him and show myself to him."
(*Jn.* 14:21 TJB). If we only obey His word, then we shall perceive
His Presence as glorified Light, even in this world. But let us refer
again to the teaching of Alvarez de Paz:

It is a very precious gift by which God manifests
Himself in the depths and inmost center of the
soul with a very strong light. He shows Himself
present, regarding the soul and tenderly loving her
... The mind knows Him, now as a certain ALL in
which all is good, now as having one or more special perfections.[9]

This supernatural Light is not like any other light that we
know upon earth. When this Light of Christ shines upon us or
within us, a powerful transforming energy flows within the deepest recesses of our being and changes our nature. It heals, strengthens, purifies, and renews people. It enlightens the intellect by
increasing our capacity to understand the mysteries of faith as
we meditate upon the Word of God in Scripture. Thus, slowly
and gently, the risen Lord draws His people into the supernatural
life of redemption.

Let us now look at the form of God's glory within the Cloud.
The Bible student will recall that Mary, the Mother of Christ, was
overshadowed at the Annunciation by the power of the Spirit. Mary,
in response to the Angel's message, pronounced her "fiat" and
shortly thereafter began to reflect the glory she received back to
the Father in her prophetic song, the Magnificat, which states: "My

Spirit exults in God my savior ... All generations shall call me blessed." (*Lk.* 1:47, 48 TJB).

Therese Neuman, the stigmatic from Konnersreuth, Germany, tells about a vision she was privileged to see concerning the Annunciation. When relating the vision, she speaks of the fact that she saw the light of glory enter into the personhood of Mary.

> When he is finished, the Virgin bows her head and says a few words. At that same moment Theresa sees a mighty light from above enter into the Virgin, while the angel after bowing once again, disappears into the air.[10]

After learning that she was to be the Mother of Christ, the spirit-filled Mary, full of praise, hastens to visit her cousin Elizabeth, who awaits the birth of John the Baptist. At the Visitation, both women are under the powerful anointing of the Holy Spirit, as is evident by their jubilant praise and prophesying. This is confirmed by the ray of light which Theresa Neuman relates in her vision of the Visitation.

> A ray of light passes from Mary to Elizabeth. Elizabeth raises her right hand and speaks some inspired words, whereupon Mary, speaking in a powerful singing tone, speaks under inspiration much longer than Elizabeth.[11]

At this point, the unborn herald of light, John the Baptist, stirs in his mother's womb as the radiant power of the hidden Christ touches his spirit and makes him leap for joy. The Spirit of God touches the human spirit and transforms the natural into the supernatural as the Lord of Glory ignited the fire of divine love within John. Is it any wonder that these two Mothers rejoiced greatly that day? And yet, what happened then is also meant to take place within the lives of all those who are members of His Body, though in a manner less grand.

St. Francis of Assisi confirms this and urges his followers to share this treasure with the beloved of Christ. He writes in one of

The Radiance of Divine Glory

his homilies,"You can know only one treasure and that is the Light of God in you. Pass it from one to another like torches in the night."[12]

Those who are one in the Spirit and are mature Christians will readily perceive and experience this sharing of the Light of glory as they minister Christ's love one to another in healing, anointing, and other works. It was a delightful surprise to find this in the life of St. Francis, for long before I had knowledge of such things the Spirit had inspired this prayer within my heart: "O Holy Spirit, enflame me until I become a torch of fire for Thee!" And this is the Fire that Jesus has come to cast upon the earth — the Fire of His Presence and the fire of His love.

Blessed Ann C. Emmerich, an Augustinian nun of the 1700's, writes in her book *The Life of the Blessed Virgin Mary* about the mystery of the Nativity which she was privileged to see in a vision. She, like St. Francis and Theresa Neuman, had the extraordinary gift of the stigmata. She has described her vision of the Nativity in this way:

> [Joseph] saw her as it were surrounded by flames, the whole cave was as if filled with supernatural light. He gazed at her like Moses when he saw the burning bush; then he went into his little room in holy awe and threw himself on his face in prayer ... It was the radiance round the Blessed Virgin ever growing greater ... The stones of the roof, of the walls, and of the floor of the cave became as it were alive in the light ... A pathway of light opened above Mary rising with ever increasing glory towards the height of heaven.[13]

God, who dwells in inaccessible light, manifested His union with Mary by transfiguring her into a vessel of light. The night of the Nativity was for Mary another Mt. Tabor, experienced in a personal way, for she was transfigured within and without by the Shakinah glory.

The same experience of God's glory that took place within the lives of Moses, St. Francis, John the Baptist, Mary, and Jesus Himself can also take place within our lives, though to a lesser

83

degree, if we imitate their whole-hearted surrender of our lives to the Father through the Spirit. Perhaps it has already taken place within your life.

It has always amazed me that when God desires to teach a person a certain truth, He invariably excites a fierce hunger, an insatiable desire, within that person's spirit to reach forth for all he is worth to grasp the Heavenly Father, who alone can satisfy that hunger. This man will feel as though he is starving, though he cannot himself understand why. The merciful Father will direct this hapless soul, as He cannot in His infinite compassion bear to see such wretchedness in one of His children. He will nourish and sustain that soul, much, I believe, as He has sustained me through the grace of contemplation and other life-renewing experiences, the climax of which is surely the experience of the Divine Glory.

It was at a time in my life when I was spiritually hungry that the Father's great love and compassion were revealed to me within a cloud of glory. This occurred immediately after I had received Holy Communion, which had made me acutely aware of His sacramental presence around me and within me. As I knelt before the tabernacle in an attempt to make a good thanksgiving, I grew keenly aware, through the spiritual senses, of Yahweh's majestic Presence before me as a column of Cloud. The majesty and power were so overwhelming that I wanted to fall on my face and hide my own unworthiness. Surely no one could stand before such magnificence. The Spirit prompted me to say, "Oh Lord, what am I in Your sight?" I don't even know why I said this, except that He desired it, for He wanted me to learn of my nothingness before Him. He did so immediately after the question by showing me that I would not even exist had He not called me into being out of nothingness. He showed me a vast empty space, a vacuum. Then the Cloud-Presence came nearer, and everything turned black. I could see nothing and was blind before Him as He caught me up into that vastness and absorbed me into it. Those who have experienced this will understand it best. The great scholar Gregory of Nyssa experienced God's Presence within this Cloud, and he describes it thus:

> Next comes a closer awareness of hidden things
> ... to the world of the invisible. And this aware-
> ness is a kind of cloud ... It accustoms the soul to
> look towards what is hidden ... She (the soul and
> spirit) enters within the secret chamber of divine
> knowledge, and here she is cut off on all sides by
> the divine darkness.[14]

Also when I searched Scripture for mention of a similar encounter with God, I came to this verse: "And he made misty-clouds
his wrap." (*Ps.* 18:12 NAB). The prophet Ezekiel wrote: "The temple
was filled with the Cloud." (*Ez.* 10:4 NAB). We also see in Exodus,
"I am coming to you in a dense cloud." (*Ex.* 19:9 TJB). Do you see
how the Spirit was teaching about His glory? His Presence? You
see, I knew very little about His Word; yet, he always sees the desire of our hearts and will lead us out of our ignorance if we let
Him. In this regard, St. Augustine describes how God revealed to
him his unworthiness and brought him to spiritual wisdom.

> Wisdom, Wisdom itself, which in those moments
> shines upon me, cleaving through my cloud. And
> the cloud returns to wrap me round once more as
> my strength is beaten down under its darkness and
> the weight of my sins; for my strength is weak-
> ened through poverty...[15]

It seems a paradox to say that God is Light so intense that He
blinds one and also that He is a Cloud of darkness. But He is both.
If a person looked directly into the sun or a bright light for even a
few moments, the brightness therein would blind him so that he
would see only darkness. St. John of the Cross speaks of this darkness of Presence.

> It leaves it not only dark, but likewise empty... The
> soul thinks not that it has this light, but believes
> itself to be in darkness, even as we have said of
> the ray of light...[16]

This is also known as blinding contemplation, wherein one is united to the Lord within a transluminous obscurity. St. Angela of Foligno describes the darkness of divine contemplation.

> And then I beheld him in the midst of darkness. I say darkness because He is a treasure of such magnitude that neither reason nor thought can grasp Him, and nothing that belongs to the world or what can be thought and grasped reach Him...
>
> Rather does this treasure overwhelm the soul with unutterable ecstasy, so that it cannot express with its mouth or even grasp with the heart all it beholds.[17]

When the Apostle Paul first encountered God, he also was blinded by this "ray of divine darkness," as it is called. The majestic Light of the Lord is overwhelming and shines upon us to transform us, even as it did Paul and so many others. Because of our sinfulness, we stand abashed before such Radiance. We can open ourselves to this Light through the purification of our inner being by repentance.

Dionysius the Areopagite, a monk who wrote at the time of the Councils of Ephesus and Chalcedon in the fifth century, explains:

> For by the unceasing and absolute renunciation of thyself and all things thou shalt in pureness cast aside, and be released from all and so shalt be led upwards to the Ray of that Divine Darkness, which exceeds all existence.[18]

This action of God's Spirit remains wrapped in obscurity because the Lord is operating secretly in the deepest recesses of the spirit. This is not only a union, but a transforming act on the part of God. John Tauler, a Dominican professor and spiritual director of contemplatives, describes this second feature of the Ray of Divine Darkness.

Then the spirit is transported high above all the faculties into a void of immense solitude whereof no mortal can adequately speak. It is the mysterious darkness wherein is concealed the limitless God.[19]

I believe this is what I was experiencing during the time when the Cloud of God's Presence showed me the immense vastness, which was really a space for encounter. During these times of infused contemplation or mystic union, the soul will find itself transported to places which only God knows. My words are inadequate again. Trust in the Spirit of the Lord to teach you, together with those who are wise in such things.

In the descriptions I have given here, I hope you can see how the Lord presents Himself before His Chosen to commission them for a particular work in building His kingdom. He will make their spirits hunger for knowledge of the Lord. Once these hungry, thirsty men and women become ready to surrender their very souls to the Father, He will then direct them in the most profound ways into the Divine Presence itself. In the schools of contemplation and hard experience, He will teach them Sanctity and Truth. By infusing His grace in them, as Power and as Light, He equips them for their respective tasks and transforms them into a whole new breed of man. Touched by the Fire of the Spirit, the very Fire of His glory, these men and women will already have been privileged with a preview of what awaits every true Christian when the Kingdom is established, for "When Christ, our life, appears then you shall appear with Him in glory." (*Col.* 3:4 NAB). What praise we should give to Him! What glory! Thanks be to God.

The Sword of the Spirit

–7–

Gifts of Healing

"Yet it was our infirmities that he bore ... and by his stripes were healed." (*Is.* 54:4,5 NAB). In these words of Scripture we note that Jesus paid the price of our sicknesses as well as our sins. Yet we have many Christians today who have not accepted His message of divine healing. What is the cause of this? Is it a lack of instruction? If so, we must raise their level of faith by teaching the words of Scripture which apply to healing and by demonstrating our own belief in healing prayer, for faith comes by healing and healing by believing. The majority of people do not yet understand that Jesus heals the body as well as the soul and therefore have not appropriated their inheritance of wholeness. They do not understand that Jesus came to redeem the whole man, not just the spiritual side of man.

When the Son of God walked the face of the earth, He bore witness to His Father's healing love for all mankind by curing diseases, healing the blind and the deaf, and by relieving all kinds of perplexing problems. He healed those in bondage by deliverance. He healed the ignorant by giving them His teachings. He healed the hungry by multiplying the loaves and fishes. He healed the grief-stricken by raising the dead. He gave everyone He met a second chance for a better life. He was the personification of healing love, and He has commissioned us to follow His example.

Before His Ascension, He told the disciples, Mary, and the holy women that He would send them the Spirit to help them. He then empowered them at Pentecost to do the same works He had done in order to build up the Kingdom. "You will receive power when the Holy Spirit comes down upon you." (*Acts* 1:8 TJB). These bearers of Christ's "good news" could be identified by certain signs which showed their incorporation into the Body of Christ. What were these identifying signs? "These are the signs that will be associated with believers: in my name they will cast out devils; they will have the gift of tongues; they will pick up snakes in their hands, and be unharmed should they drink deadly poison; they will lay their hands on the sick, who will recover." (*Mk.* 16:18 TJB). We have the word of Christ that believers will be empowered to heal through the life giving power of God's Spirit.

Since the living word of God is an eternal word, we see that the truths given mankind two thousand years ago by Christ are applicable today. We know, therefore, that the Lord expects His followers to continue His healing work in the modern world. Healing has always been a regularly exercised ministry in the Apostolic Church, but it has only been within the last thirty years that its reappearance has been witnessed in large Christian gatherings. With each succeeding year there has been an increasing number of believers who have come into the healing ministry. I believe that the reason for this is that we have entered into the age of the Parousia, or the Messianic Age; hence, the unprecedented anointing of flesh with God's Spirit.

For hundreds of years it was not a common practice for lay people, single or married, to minister healing prayers unto others. But as the Lord is pouring forth the latter rain of the Spirit upon all flesh, we see an emergence of those who are endowed with a healing ministry. This appears to be a new concept within the Church, but it was a patristic practice to use unordained elders for healing ministries within their Christian communities. At present there is much misunderstanding about lay ministries, but there is an excellent book which deals with the problems of these ministries. This controversial book sheds light upon these present-day problems and is an invaluable aid to a better understanding of this situation. The book, *Unordained Elders and Renewal Communities*, by Steve Clark, is published by Paulist Press.

If the Christians of today appropriate and put into practice the scriptural teachings about healing, I believe that divine healing will become a daily blessing in the Church. Our task is to open our minds and hearts to the teachings of Christ and to imitate the example of our fathers, the early patriarchs.

Let us continue now to meditate upon the Word. "Let your heart treasure what I have to say." (*Prov.* 4:4 TJB). "If one of you is ill, he should send for the elders of the church, and they must anoint him with oil in the name of the Lord." (*James* 5:14 TJB). As believers who took these words to heart and acted upon them, my own family was blessed with many healings. And when other people heard about them, they began to ask for prayers for their own various needs.

As we began to minister to the sick, we found that those who bore resentments or hated others had to seek forgiveness of their brothers or sisters in Christ, as well as God's, because oftentimes their lack of forgiveness prevented them from receiving healing. They had to make at least an attempt to repair broken relationships through reconciliation as Jesus taught: "If you do not forgive others, neither will your Father forgive you." (*Matt.* 6:15 NAB). Their attitude of forgiveness should reflect that of the crucified Christ, whose last words were, "Father, forgive them..." (*Lk.* 23:24 TJB). We found that leading others into reconciliation often insured the total well-being of the person. We gave others the example in Scripture where Jesus healed the sick man as He simultaneously forgave him his sins: "Be sure not to sin anymore or something worse may happen to you." (*Jn.* 5:14-15 TJB).

The Divine Physician has created mankind to live according to specific laws which regulate their intricate beings. The framework of His laws is love, and those who refuse to live within this framework of His design become disoriented within their being. This disorientation then becomes externalized physically through sickness and internalized spiritually through a lessening of the God-life within. Thus they are weakened and become easy prey to evil spirits, which can wreak havoc in body, mind, soul, and spirit. The only remedy in such cases is to repent of wrong-doing and return to God's original plan for us.

Many people erroneously believe that healing applies to only one area of the human make-up, such as physical healing or spiritual healing. But there are as many types of healing as there are illnesses, and this would include all physiological and emotional needs. We found through our experiences that some people who had mental conditions were healed through a prayer of "deliverance." The Lord sent His followers into the world to set the captives free, and this would include those who were in the bondage of mental oppression. We found that people were freed by taking authority over the spirits who were causing the mental condition.

Great caution and discernment must be exercised in these cases, for the root cause in each illness differs. The deliverance ministry should not be attempted by those who are immature Christians lest great harm be done. Although many do not believe that evil forces can cause sickness, depression, and suicidal tendencies, there are numerous examples of such cases. The Lord expects us to turn to Him in all our needs.

When the believers prayed for healing, they laid their hands upon the sick, thereby following the example of the Master, who gave healing and blessing through the touch of His hands. Touching in this manner signifies more than just an external expression of loving concern. This touch establishes the spiritual contact through which Christ transmits His life-giving power into the person seeking to be restored. We become like electrical wires transmitting a new life-force into the recipient. Some of us will be able to conduct more of this power than others, of course. Each person has a different capacity to minister according to his nature.

Electricity, I have found, is a very spiritual metaphor for the experience of healing through the Spirit. Frequently there is the sensation of a Fire burning within one's spirit, radiating energy or heat. At other times, it will feel as if live wires are running beneath the surface of the skin of one's arms and hands. One will also feel the life-force coming through the pores of the skin. Although these various sensations usually confirm that the restorative healing power is being bestowed to others, it is not altogether important that it be experienced. It is not necessary to expect such phenomena in the act of healing, for the Lord often uses various ways in which to work.

The reception of the Sacraments is also a tremendous avenue whereby the Lord works to strengthen the whole person. When properly received, the Sacraments can become very effective channels of healing, for they reaffirm our relationship with God. To neglect the Sacraments is to neglect a sanctifying encounter with the Healer Himself. We receive spiritual healing through Penance, spiritual nourishment through Holy Communion, and oftentimes spiritual and physical healing through the Anointing of the Sick. I have myself, during Holy Communion, experienced the healing of a large cyst. My doctor examined me at a later date and was amazed that it had disappeared.

The more I progressed in the understanding of divine healing, the more I discovered the miraculous power of Jesus' name. This name, which is above all names, reveals Christ's mission as the "Savior" who would redeem the world by restoring it to the perfect plan which the Father designed. We have used the holy name of Jesus to bring forth the power of healing, of deliverance, and every type of conceivable blessing. The Father takes delight in His Son and bestows a blessing every time His Son's name is pronounced. The reverent use of His name in prayer becomes the springboard of the Spirit's activity. Can you see now why the pagans and enemies of Christ in apostolic days forbade the believers to use this name? They realized that the powerful name of Jesus invoked power in blessings.

The Spirit, who is our greatest teacher and consoler, began to reveal to us the restorative power contained within the use of Jesus' name in certain life-and-death situations. As I have said, the Spirit inspired us to have prayer meetings within our home, and immediately all kinds of trials began to take place. The spiritual warfare had begun. On the appointed day of our first meeting, a crisis took place which nearly took the life of our baby. He was happily playing in the room when suddenly he began to choke and was gasping for breath. He began to turn blue in the face, and I realized that if he could not breathe he might have brain damage for lack of oxygen. I tried in every way to help him, but to no avail. I ran outdoors with him in my arms, hoping to get a ride to the hospital. As I ran down the driveway, I cried out in anguish, "Oh, Jesus, Jesus!" Almost immediately the bluish pallor began to fade from his face, and he began to breathe normally again. Meanwhile a neighbor had called an ambulance, and we drove off to the hospital to have him checked. Apparently he had not swallowed anything. Though the cause of this accident remained a mystery to us, we all knew that the Lord had helped by my calling upon His powerful name. We returned home witnessing to what the Lord had done.

The Lord continued to teach me about healing through various emergencies and crises where there was no alternative but to reach out to Him in faith and ask for healing love. It was in this way that I discovered the power of healing as it is described in the Bible. Many of these situations which He placed me in were absolutely terrifying. But it was precisely this type of situation that brought forth the prayer of faith as never before.

One of these events took place with an automobile accident in front of our home. A boy had ridden his tricycle into the street, into the pathway of an approaching car. There was a head-on collision, and the child was thrown into the air. I just happened to be looking out the window when it happened, and my heart was pounding as I ran to the child, who was lying motionless on the curb in a large pool of blood. "Was he alive?" I asked myself. The whole side of his head was opened, and he was rapidly losing blood. Terrified for his life, I cried out, "Father, in the name of Jesus, stop this blood from flowing out!" Immediately the blood stopped, almost as if Someone had turned off a faucet. I could barely look upon this pitiful sight, but continued to pray for him in the Spirit, for I did not know if he was breathing. The ambulance arrived, and the attendants handed me thick bandages to place under the boy's head as they looked on hopelessly. When the attendants were about to put him into the ambulance, the boy astonished everyone by regaining consciousness. He did not cry or complain about his injuries, in spite of the fact that his head was gashed open from the temple to the crown. He was placed into the ambulance and rushed away. Later we learned that he had sustained a broken shoulder, internal injuries, and a possible concussion. In spite of all this, he was healed in a short time, and in two days he was released from the hospital.

A witness of the accident, who was a high school teacher, made this remark about the boy's condition: "I've seen people bleed to death like that in just a minute or two." An investigating attorney came to inquire about the accident, and I asked his opinion about the case and if he thought that anything supernatural had happened here. He noted that the boy had been critically injured, and he believed that the Lord had healed him. This attorney was not a Christian believer, but from the facts he gathered he knew that what had happened was most unusual. My faith in healing prayer grew tremendously because of this accident.

It seemed as if a regular series of emergencies evolved to test and strengthen our belief in healing grace. You see, at this time the only healings or miracles we had ever heard of had taken place at famous shrines. The extent of the healing ministry in our area was nil. Can you see how the Lord was teaching us about healing through this school of harsh experience?

In still another case, illness called the faith of my family into action. Since the year 1957 my husband had suffered a spinal condition which required surgery. He had to wear a back brace, take medication, and was hospitalized several times a year. One day the curvature became acutely painful, and his physician was out of town. This was the only doctor who was able to help him, and my husband had to work but could not even stand up.

By this time we had learned the power of praise, and so we gathered the family together to praise the Lord for this problem. Does this sound strange? I guess it would to those without faith. We began by singing hymns to the Lord and then, laying our hands upon my husband, asked the Lord in Jesus' name to heal his back, just as the Bible instructs us to do. Shortly afterwards, in the midst of prayer, my husband began to laugh and laugh. He said, "I know I'm healed," and he stood up as straight as a rail. Well, he has not had any more serious trouble after all these years. Our joy in the Lord knew no limits.

We had no doubts about praying for healing from this time on, for the Lord had given us sufficient proof that His healing grace was always available. In our household there are seven children, and those with children know how frequently they are beset with illnesses or accidents. One day our youngest child had a temperature of 105 and went into a convulsion. It was Sunday afternoon and no doctors were available, so we gathered for praise and the laying on of hands. The child came out of the convulsions, fell asleep, and within two hours his temperature returned to normal — without medication.

With such a large family as ours, accidents seemed always to be happening. One day my daughter's kneecap became dislocated just as we were going out to give a witness talk. She was crying because of the intense pain. Touching her knee, in Jesus' name we asked the Lord in prayer to heal her. Suddenly there was a loud cracking sound, and the bone was in place. She quickly dried her tears and returned to her game. At another time, a small bone in the foot was dislocated, and again with prayer it went back into place. The Lord gave us so much proof that He really cares about His children and wants to relieve even the smallest discomfort.

Another child had bad eyesight. We attended a prayer meeting and asked the Lord to heal his eyes. During the meeting he looked up and said, "Mommy, my eyes feel like they are burning." I told him to continue praying for a while with his eyes closed. When he opened them, he said that all objects in the room looked closer to him. His eyesight was improved, and he began to believe in the Lord in a new way. The doctor told us his vision had improved 80 percent. But even more important, this youngster had experienced the love of God in a personal way.

Through all these experiences we have come to believe the same words which were spoken to the Israelites so long ago: "I, the Lord, am your healer." (*Ex.* 15:26 NAB). We believed and acted upon the words Jesus spoke: "The sick upon whom they lay hands will recover." (*Mk.* 16:18 NAB).

The works of healing first occurred within our own family and circle of friends. Then it began to broaden into the public. My husband owned a barber business and asked me to work with him. Although I did not care to do this type of work, I agreed to help and discovered that it was part of God's providential plan. Many times people would come to the shop with needs that required healing and they would ask our help or prayers. It was quite natural to speak to our customers about the Lord and what He had done in our lives. A man who had been a boxer for several years was seeking to know the Lord, and this opened the door to a discussion about the love of Christ, sickness, and sin. We explained that if he renewed his baptismal promises and received Jesus as His Lord, he would experience a new life of faith. As we prayed for Don, he experienced the infilling of the Holy Spirit and began to weep, as he was overwhelmed by the power of God's love. We did not know that Don needed physical healing, but the Lord healed him of severe migraines when he received the baptism of the Spirit. Don never suffered again from them.

The Lord cares about the smallest bruises, as well as the terminal illnesses and serious health problems. His word tells us to pray for each other to be healed, and so we continued to obey His word. An old friend, who had an enlarged heart with damaged blood vessels, also asked us to pray for her heart. We said a simple prayer, and she left to go on a trip. While she was gone, she became ill and visited her doctor. He was concerned about her heart condition, so he took some medical pictures of her heart. In the meantime, we were unaware of what had happened. When he saw the pictures, he could not believe it. Her previously enlarged heart had been restored to normal, and the damaged vessels were in perfect condition. The doctor was astounded by this miracle, and determined to write a medical paper on her case in the near future. When the woman returned home, she called us to tell us what Jesus had done for her in answer to prayer. Needless to say, she was overjoyed. The Lord's promise was true; He said, "If you remain in me ... you may ask what you will and you shall get it." (*Jn.* 15:7 TJB).

The list of healings we have experienced could go on and on; but there were many times when we prayed and nothing seemed to happen, at least on the surface. Many times the Lord will do a deep spiritual work instead of a physical healing, and that is not always obvious at the beginning. I don't think that anyone should ever stop praying for healing if he does not get immediate results. There is a time and season for all things. God hears our prayers, but He does not always answer them in the way we expect. He always gives more blessings than we ask for.

The dawn of each new day became another exciting adventure in Christ. The Spirit of the Lord brought many needy people into our lives. We were poor among the poor and could empathize with them in every way. We understood the reality of the beatitude of the poor in Spirit, for we had no one to lean upon except the Lord, and we thank Him for that great lesson in poverty. He therefore became our source of knowledge and of love, our source of understanding and compassion. We did not attend a school to learn about ministry, for the Word of God taught us. We learned through the inspirations of the Spirit and through our experience in praying for healing that Jesus, the Healer, is waiting for those who reach out to Him for wholeness. We strove to bring others to this awareness, and those who could grasp this found that many of their needs were met when they submitted their lives to the Lord.

And the exciting awareness of Christ's fabulous love for mankind grew to unexpected heights. Hundreds of people received the baptism of the Spirit and were physically healed in the process. A clergyman who suffered from internal hemorrhage was restored to perfect health within a short time after receiving the release of the Spirit. He had not been expected to live, but he is now working full time in his parish.

Several people who were healed through our ministry sent us letters acknowledging their healing. Their testimonies are included here in the following.

Oct. 29, 1977

To Whom It May Concern:

I, Harry Plummer of 211 Morris Ave., Girard, Ohio, had a bad skin rash since I was in the armed service for twenty-five years. I spent thousands of dollars for a cure which I did not receive.

The morning that I came to get a haircut, I was very uncomfortable from the skin rash. I met Audrey A. Mrofchak, who works with her husband and we discussed the power of prayer for healing. I told her that I truly believed in healing, however, she did not know that I had a problem. I did not disclose my problem, but I definitely needed help. So she told me that she often prayed for healing and the baptism of the spirit and asked if I wanted prayer. We prayed together along with Paul Mrofchak, Sr., and within a few days my skin rash was completely healed. I do not need medication any longer, nor do I see a physician any longer. I feel that the Lord touched me spiritually and physically.

> Sincerely,
> Harry T. Plummer
> 211 Morris Ave.
> Girard, Ohio 44420

> Oct. 12, 1977
> 2874 Trumbul Ave.
> Mc Donald, Ohio

Dear Audrey,

I couldn't wait to tell you what happened as a result of your prayers for healing several weeks ago.

I'll try to explain it as I understand it. Five years ago, in 1972, I had a bladder operation because I was very sick. Several months ago I began to have a constant pain which lasted for two weeks, so I thought I should see my doctor again. He examined me and said, "You are full of adhesions and will need another operation because of the pain it is causing."

I was afraid because I didn't want to return to the hospital again. When you laid hands on me to pray for healing, I felt numb all over and was much like those who are "slain in the spirit" for about an hour. I hardly felt conscious and, try as I may, I could not move or get up. Never had I ever experienced such a things as this.

Several days later, while I was at home, I noticed the pain was all gone. Once more, I saw my doctor and he was amazed as he examined me. He couldn't understand what happened but he told me

I would no longer have need of the operation.
Praise & thank God.

Sincerely,
Emma Luknis

Because the Christian belongs to Christ, he is one with Him and becomes the instrument of the Holy Spirit to accomplish the same works that Jesus did, such as healing and freeing the oppressed who are in bondage. Because the believer is part of the militant Body of Christ upon earth, he or she is called to participate in the ministry of healing and spiritual warfare by using the gifts and the power of His Spirit to fight against "the rules of this world of darkness." (*Eph.* 6:12 NAB).

We saw that Jesus walked throughout the land healing "all who were in the grip of the devil." (*Acts* 11:38 NAB), rebuking evil spirits and curing illnesses. He rebuked the fever in Peter's mother-in-law; He cast out the unclean; He cured the deaf and the dumb in order to heal others. The disciples ministered in the same way by casting out all evil powers such as the spirits of infirmity, the spirits of divination, the seducing spirits, the lying spirits. We are exhorted by St. Paul to "draw your strength from the Lord" and "stand firm against the tactics of the devil." (*Eph.* 6:11,12 NAB). The Word tells the believer to resist the devil and all his evil spirits. To resist here means to oppose evil forces, to fight them with the weapons of God. The first deceitful tactic these evil forces use victory over sin and death and that His victory is ours. The Lord said, "Use my name to expel demons." (*Mk.* 16:17 NAB).

As believers of the word, we found that when we stood firm upon His promises and claimed them, He responded to us by honoring our prayers time after time. He began to teach us about deliverance, as we strove to walk in His light.

It began like this. The chaplain of a nearby hospital asked us to visit a mentally distressed patient whose condition remained a problem because no one had been successful in determining its fundamental cause. When we talked to him, he was receptive to the healing message of Christ in Scripture. We prayed that the Lord would disclose to us the root cause of his distress. We asked

Jesus to give us a word from the Bible, and we were led to this passage: "This man has an unclean spirit." I was hesitant to disturb the privacy of his consciousness, but decided that his well-being was important enough to risk tactful probing. This man readily confessed that he indeed had been oppressed by numerous unclean thoughts and images for many years. Now, he was a disciplined Christian man; but although he tried, he was unable to dislodge these images from his mind. These "hideous thoughts" were slowly driving him to the point of complete breakdown, and he was powerless to help himself. This person was not acquainted with the ministry of deliverance and was unable to discern or cast out the unclean spirit which had invaded his mind and caused this mental quirk. My husband and I, realizing through prayer what must be done, took authority over the unclean spirit in the power of Jesus' name and told it to leave the man, never to return. Almost immediately the terrible depression which had held this man in bondage was broken by the sword of His Spirit — the Word of God. The healing power of the Savior touched him, and he quickly regained his equanimity and was released from the hospital. The Chaplain later confirmed that this person had indeed been set free from physical and mental oppression.

This was our first lesson in deliverance. Now when I write about deliverance, I am not referring to people who are possessed by demons, but of those who are oppressed in certain areas of their lives, such as those who are addicted or bound by certain vices. The believer has been instructed to set the captives free, but few have yet realized that this Gospel message was meant to apply to the whole Body of Christ, in whom the Spirit lives.

I came to realize this message within the situations which came up daily and within prayer meetings. One night a very depressed young man came to me at a meeting and whispered in my ear that he was going to commit suicide. He pleaded, "Help me before it's too late." I quietly led him to a corner so that after the meeting was over we could talk about his problem. We talked, and I led him to the point where he was willing to pray with me and rebuke the evil spirit which bound him with a lethal depression and instilled in him the thought to destroy himself. He went into spasms, which indicated a terrible struggle in his inner being, but within ten minutes the stronghold had been taken and the despair lifted. The young man confessed that he had felt something leave him and that the suicidal thoughts had now disappeared. He knew that the Lord had done this, and he was now "looking forward to a new life." He later received the baptism of the Spirit and became a great witness for Christ among his high school students.

More and more often I encountered situations where deliverance was needed. At an out-of-state prayer group, a priest I had met requested that I talk with "Joe" in order to discern the cause of a problem he suffered with. I agreed to try. Three priests, Joe, and I met privately to pray, and the Lord gave me discernment into Joe's problem. He was in need of healing in three areas: the healing of the memory and of the heart — and the spiritual healing of the soul, through repentance and deliverance. Joe had formerly been a brother in a religious order but had left, and his life was a maze of confusion. He had traveled all the way from Ireland to seek help. After the Lord had given us discernment of his problem, Joe agreed to confess his wrong doing in the Sacrament of Confession. After that, the priests asked me to pray for deliverance, at which time the four spirits which had held him in bondage many years were rebuked, and he was finally released. I then ministered with him for the healing of memories and the heart. Christ had set him free, and this new-found freedom was evident in his joy. The priests in attendance had never witnessed this type of healing before, and they themselves asked in prayer for the release of the charismatic gifts, which they all did receive.

That day was unique in so many ways that it will always remain outstanding in my mind. The Jesuit was on his way to Scotland; Joe was to return to Ireland. They agreed to meet in Ireland to establish a Christian community there. The two diocesan priests and a few lay people who were with them were to return to the East Coast of America with the hope of establishing a prayer group in their area. We heard from them regularly, and within three years this small group had established not one, but ninety prayer groups in the New England states. We could not praise the Lord enough to show our thanksgiving.

After these initial experiences in deliverance, the Lord arranged another situation in which He taught me about achieving deliverance from a distance. A friend asked if I would pick up a relative at a nearby airport. I agreed to meet this relative, but was somewhat troubled, for I was acquainted with the undisciplined lifestyle of this person and realized that he needed spiritual help. As I drove to this destination, I prayed and was once more given the discernment of his bondage. When I began to rebuke certain evil spirits within this person, my car started to swerve back and forth across the road, yet I was not turning the steering wheel. A large semi-truck was approaching and I was scared. I could not believe what was happening to the car. Some invisible force moved the car at will. Then suddenly I remembered something. I had neglected to bind the evil spirits verbally and pray for divine protection. Immediately I cried out, "Jesus, protect me! I bind you, evil spirits, in the name of Jesus." At once the car was again under my control and I went merrily on my way, continuing in prayer. Upon arriving at the airport, I could see a definite change in the person I met there.

Later I asked a very holy and learned man his opinion about the incident, and he told me that I should not worry, since the poltergeists were only trying to frighten me so that, out of fear, I would not utter that prayer of deliverance. They try to inhibit God's people through fear so that the believer does not take authority over them. But Jesus' eternal word tells us that the believer is able to cast out demons. The Lord has repeatedly given us prophetic words telling us to break through the bondage His people are in. The greatest deception and bondage that Satan uses is the iron chain of fear and disbelief in the word of God, which teaches that the believer can rebuke and cast out evil spirits in the name of Jesus. The Lord has extended this power to those who are in His Body upon earth by means of His indwelling Holy Spirit. If the Christian cannot grasp this, he will be defenseless and conquered by the mere fact that he will not use the weapons of spiritual warfare that Christ has designated for that purpose. The Lord told His people to resist the devil, to oppose him, to fight against him. He would not have given us His word without the power to accomplish the task of freeing the oppressed.

Daily we became more astonished at the works Jesus accomplished in answer to prayer. We saw that in cases of drug addiction the people involved were healed through deliverance and healing prayer. They had to surrender their lives to the Divine Physician, who alone knows how to bring about a restoration of the whole person. This healing is not a momentary thing, but should be an ongoing process involving Christian teaching, support, and brotherhood. According to statistics, only two percent of habitual drug users are ever healed through medicine and hospitalization, whereas those healed in the context of a charismatic renewal are of a much higher percentage rate.

I have seen critical cases of drug abuse where patients had lapsed into comas, but were still revived through prayer in the Spirit. Take the case of a teenage girl who had taken a hard drug, lapsed into a coma, and was rushed to the hospital; she went into respiratory arrest and had to be given oxygen. Needless to say, here was a very serious condition. I had been called to go and pray with her. Upon arriving at the emergency ward, I anointed her with holy oil and, laying hands upon her, prayed that her life would be spared and that the Lord would heal her of drug abuse and any bad effects from this incident. Her life hung in the balance for five hours, but Scripture tells us to persist in prayer, and so I did. She began to stir slightly and partially regained consciousness; it was then that I asked her to call upon the powerful name of Jesus to heal her. She did this, and within a few more hours, regained total consciousness. Her breathing returned to normal, and she was in a healthy state once more. The doctors were just amazed that she recovered so quickly. They could not understand it. However, the effect of Christ's healing love was evident to those who believed. In this case, persistent prayer seemed to be the deciding factor. Spiritual warfare is not to be taken lightly, especially when a life hangs in the balance. Many people believe that it is impossible for drug addiction to be cured, but nothing is impossible where the Lord is concerned.

I can tell of other cases of drug addicts who were sincerely seeking help, were willing to repent of their wrong-doing, and were ready to rebuke the oppressing spirits. But this spirit of reform is just the beginning. These people need meeting places or schools where they can be trained in Christian values so that they can learn to rely upon the Lord instead of on drugs when times get rough. When the addict is ready to yield to the Lord's way, He never turns away, but pours out blessings upon those who commit their lives to

Him. What tremendous witnesses several of these addicts have become when they proclaim the Lord as their Healer.

Please remember that all the healings described in this chapter took place within the scope of our lives as ordinary lay people who are not particularly talented or generally known as healers. The simple fact that one believes in God's word and has yielded to the operation of the gifts of the Holy Spirit makes one a candidate for the healing experience. The *Acts of the Apostles* tells us that the disciples and Apostles were just ordinary people, too, until they received the Holy Spirit on Pentecost. It was at Pentecost that they became committed servants, anointed vessels, living temples, and stewards of the manifold gifts of God.

Today, as in days gone by, the Lord Jesus Christ still seeks those who are willing to be channels of His love in healing, reconciliation, and ministries of all kinds. The necessary qualification is total surrender to Jesus as Lord; then watch the Spirit move in your daily life.

The sign of the time, for example, the New Pentecost, is an indication that the Lord is no longer satisfied with a small group of committed disciples here and there. It seems rather that He is in the process of calling forth the holy nation, His royal priesthood, who will minister unto Him and to His world as described in *Revelation* 5. The fact that the Spirit is being poured out in abundance upon lay people in all countries tells us that something very significant is happening in our day. Fifteen years ago there were very few "healers" ministering to people. Today, lay people are praying for healing in an unprecedented way, and God is answering their prayers. These are the ones who bear the signs of the believer.

And what are the signs of the believers? Scripture tells us, "These are the signs that will be associated with believers: in my name they will cast out devils..." (*Mk.* 16:17 TJB). By the Word "believers" is meant the whole Body of believers, not just a certain few. If this were not true, the Lord would certainly have made it clear and indicated that only a few would have these signs. Scripture is quite specific in this regard.

It is an interesting and revealing fact that there is no mention of the office of "exorcist" in the various lists given in the New Testament. There are "healers," "evangelists," and "prophets," but apparently no exorcists...

They are mentioned in a list of so-called "minor orders," in a letter of Bishop Cornelius of Rome ... in 252 A.D. The office is now extinct in the Western Church, and in the Eastern, "exorcism" is regarded as a charismatic gift not attached to an office.

Again, we notice that it was Philip, a "layman," as some would call him, who cast many evil spirits out of the Samaritans. (*Acts* 8).[2]

We notice in the example of Philip, the role that the laity had in the ministry of deliverance in the Early Church. My husband and I, both lay people, have witnessed to the fact that we have experienced many healings in answer to prayer. We believe that these gifts were meant for the whole Body of Christ.

My prayer is that the Church will soon open wide their doors to the age-old concept that the Lord used the laity and unordained elders in the past and is still doing so today, though on a minor scale. The world is in great need of all kinds of healing and the workers are few. Lord, let your laborers come forth to bring about the restoration of the whole person, in every nation in the world. In Jesus' name we pray that this be done and that your holy nation come forth empowered with the healing love of Christ crucified.

–8–

Prayer of Suffering

> If anyone wants to be a follower of mine, let him renounce himself and take up his cross and follow me. (*Matt.* 16:24 TJB)

Those who follow Christ's instructions to deny themselves and take up a life of the Spirit must of necessity take up a cross before they can truly conform to His image. Some may argue that when Christ died and rose again, His work was finished. In a sense that is true, but our work as His people is not yet complete. We are urged to take up the cross and follow.

The first men who followed the Lord bearing their heavy crosses were the two thieves who died on Calvary with Him. They were not believers, yet one was to attain salvation that very day. What was the difference between the two men which brought one to salvation but not the other? Surely it was the gift of discernment, evident when the good thief rebuked his fellow by saying, "Have you no fear of God at all?" (*Lk.* 23:40 TJB). The good thief became a saint because he kept his eyes upon the Suffering Servant and learned, by watching, the proper meaning of suffering. As he suffered in imitation of the only begotten Son, he became himself transformed as an adopted son of God, reborn upon the cross. Christ therefore assured him of salvation: "Indeed, I promise you . . . today you will be with me in paradise." (*Lk.* 23:43 TJB). The bad thief, in turn, abused Christ, mocked Him, and rebelled against his cross. He did not realize the value of Christ's suffering, nor the power of the Cross. "The language of the cross" St. Paul tells us, "may be illogical to those who are not on the way to salvation, but those of us who are on the way see it as God's power to save." (*1 Cor.* 1:18 TJB).

Through the eyes of the Spirit I see on the top of Mount Calvary the most momentous battle ever fought in human history, the battle against everlasting death. I see each of the three men hanging upon their crosses as representatives of the eternal forces engaged in this archetypal struggle. Christ, as the God-man, represents all that is heavenly and good. The good thief is the representative of fallen mankind, of Adam who stole from the Tree of Knowledge in the Garden. Spiritually and humanly, he is weak, but repentant. On the other hand, the bad thief is the son of the evil one, unrepentant, rebellious, and diabolical in nature. In his curses and blasphemies he brings forth the evil nature entombed within his hard heart. Unwilling to submit to his pitiable state and unable to sacrifice himself to justice, he was diabolically determined to thwart the divine Sacrifice being offered by the Son of Heaven for all sinful men and women, this being the triumph of justice and love.

It is as if in grim parody, the son of Satan had mounted the cross in order to negate and falsify the saving action of the Crucifixion. But in spite of this, the Cross of Christ proved the more powerful. The gates of Paradise were opened to fallen men, and that promise extended to all succeeding generations.

But the bad thief was not alone in his mockery of the Crucified Lord. With him were the passers-by, the priests and the elders, all crying, "Let him save himself!" (*Lk.* 23:35 TJB). It was as if the world, in imitation of the evil one, resisted Redemption. In its fallen state, ignorant of what it was doing, it turned from Him in one mighty attempt to throw off its destiny. Even the earth quaked in protest. It was a solitary battle Christ fought against His tortured flesh, the mockery of the world, and the power of Satan. But the flesh, the world, and Sin were from the beginning willed by Heaven to failure, even though they would for a short time seem triumphant.

"Now the hour has come for the Son of Man to be glorified." (*Jn.* 12:23 TJB). Jesus glorified the Father through His obedience and suffering. And the Father was soon to glorify His Son.

Now Christ's struggle was surely a tremendous one; but so was the trial of the good thief, who was alone in his defense of the Savior against the world. No other, not even John, the one Apostle to follow the Master to the Cross, dared speak up in His defense. Surely it must have been because God opened his tortured eyes to see the true meaning of the drama being played out before him that he so spoke. Surely he was granted special graces to suffer in union with the Savior, who, you recall, cried out against being abandoned and alone, and finally to walk with Him into Paradise. Thus the good thief, who bore the image of the Crucified One in this special way, will be remembered not only as the first saint of the New Testament, but also a prototype of all those who "take up the Cross of Christ."

In the Early Church it was St. Paul who preached the message of the Cross. Throughout his ministry he bore the cross of contradiction, persecution, and loneliness. He knew that the one condition of following Christ was self-denial. It is the prayer of suffering upon which the early Church was founded. But how many Christians today are willing to accept these conditions? How many pretend to go about the work of Christ, but will not deny themselves and try to evade their crosses? Jesus Himself prayed to be relieved of the burden of Calvary, but He conquered this inclination through prayer and submitted to the will of the Father. "Am I not," he said, "to drink the cup that the Father has given me?" (*Jn.* 18:11 TJB).

The Apostles did not understand this, as they did not understand the perfect harmony that existed between Father and Son. They lacked wisdom and trust. Because they could not see the value of suffering, every time they were tested by hunger or storm they would become fearful and grumble. Always, Jesus would miraculously calm them. Even so, in the hour of greatest trial, they fled. But Jesus had a different understanding. When He spoke of His impending death, He spoke of it at times as a life-sustaining food. (*Jn.* 4:35). In this, He showed His wisdom. "It is a wisdom that none of the masters of this age have known, or they would not have crucified the Lord of Glory." (*1 Cor.* 2:8,9 TJB).

The Lord has shown us the way of the cross and expects us to identify with His suffering and death as a means of atonement; thus, we "share in His glory." (*Rm.* 8:17 NAB). When He asks of us, "Can you drink the cup that I must drink or be baptized with the baptism with which I must be baptized?" He is speaking to the Body of believers throughout the ages. (*Mk.* 10:38,39 TJB). St. Louis DeMontfort emphasized the wisdom of the Cross when he wrote:

> The Cross is, to my belief, the greatest secret of the King, the greatest mystery of Eternal Wisdom.
> I have conquered my enemies by the Cross. You will also conquer by this sign.
> Since it was necessary for Eternal Wisdom to enter heaven by the way of suffering it is necessary for you to enter by the same way.[1]

It was through an interior vision and a supernatural word that the Lord taught the value of the Cross. He showed me a young girl walking along a country road in the warm summertime. I was that young girl, and as I slowly walked along, I admired a lovely summer landscape. Suddenly, something unusual caught my eye at the edge of the road; it was a small picket fence. But no, at second glance I saw it was not a fence at all, but hundreds of tiny crosses with arms touching so that they appeared to be a fence. I stood there wondering what this could mean, and they suddenly all fell down. The tiny crosses changed before my eyes into precious stones — diamonds, rubies, pearls — scattered all over. I started to pick up as many of them as I could, and placed them in my apron. Then it all vanished.

The meaning was clear. This was the road of life along which we travel. It is filled with numerous daily trials, hardships, sufferings, and contradictions. Though we do not see it at first, these crosses are of great value, provided we pick them up. They are the jewels out of which the Lord fashions the robes and the crowns of the saints in the heavenly Jerusalem. "When the chief Shepherd appears you will win for yourselves the unfading crown of glory." (*1 Pt.* 5:4 NAB).

This vision taught me that our crosses should be received with thanksgiving, as a tremendous opportunity to become more like Christ in His sufferings as in His glory. He was likewise teaching me that my way would be strewn with crosses. As a child I knew the heavy weight of the cross, but not that with His help it could be made lighter and more sweet. Surely those who long to be united to Jesus should ask for a love of the Cross, since one will not encounter Him without encountering it. The Lord will then give us consolations and favors to help sustain us in His footsteps.

These are the various forms of contemplative prayer. Of these helps, St. Theresa of Avila writes,

> I feel certain ... that these favours are given us to strengthen our weakness ... so that we may be able to imitate Him in His great sufferings.[2]

But one must not think that accepting a life in the Spirit will free one of sorrow. Even the just men like Job speak of their suffering: "In the anguish of my spirit I must speak, lament in the bitterness of my soul." (*Jb.* 7:11 TJB). Be assured that when you have many crosses, you know that the Father loves you, because He purges every one of His sons.

God bestowed a greater favor on the Apostles and Martyrs when He gave them His Cross to carry in their humiliations, their privations, their cruel torments, than when He conferred upon them the gift of miracles and the graces necessary for the conversion of souls. All those to whom Eternal Wisdom communicated Himself were desirous of the Cross.[3]

St. Rose of Lima also had many trials to bear in her life, and asked the Lord why she was treated in this way. He explained it to her this way:

> With great attention He divided among the souls as many blessings as He had given them afflictions ... This done, the Savior raised His voice and said with majesty: Know that the grace corresponds to tribulation. This is the one true scale of Paradise.[4]

Many times one will be called upon to suffer as an intercessor for others. This type of prayer can be agonizing. I came to understand this kind of suffering when I prayed daily for fifteen years in intercession for my father. I often felt defeated, but one day the merciful hand of God touched his heart. He returned to the Lord after a lifetime of separation by repenting of his wrong-doing, going to church, and receiving the Sacrament of Reconciliation. From that day his life style changed so dramatically that he seemed a different man. And out of this conversion came so many wonderful things that it is hard not to believe it was all part of God's beautiful plan.

For example, several years later he contracted a terminal illness, and we had to nurse him at home. One night towards the end of his life, the whole family gathered around him for the laying on of hands and prayer. We prayed for four hours. The next morning he jumped out of bed and chirped, "I feel like I've been born again!" We were dumbfounded, because for the entire week previous he could not talk or move, or even breathe without difficulty. But now he found the strength to praise God.

He later died in great peace in my arms, but this was not to be the end of the matter. One day my son was speaking about him to a priest who was visiting in a nearby town. This clergyman was a stranger to this area and did not know us. Although he did not know us he asked my son, "Is your grandfather's name Edward Samuel Augustine?" Surprised, my son asked him how he knew this, and he replied, "I see him with the eyes of God." This was the sign we had been waiting for that Dad was with the Lord. "Happy are those who mourn; they shall be comforted." (*Matt.* 5:5 TJB). Death had lost its sting through the salvation which comes from the Savior.

As we yield ourselves to the Holy Spirit, we find that we can reach out to others who have great needs. We do not always realize the depths of love we can feel for others. Many times I would find myself weeping and lamenting because a soul was in dire need. As Jesus wept over Jerusalem because He did not wish to see it destroyed, so do we weep and intercede in order that these souls may find the comfort of the Lord. Like Joel, who was prompted by the Spirit, we should cry out, "Spare your people, Yahweh! Do not make your heritage a thing of shame." (*Jl.* 2:17 TJB).

Suffering in intercession for others identifies us even more closely with Christ, who interceded for all mankind upon the Cross. Actually, though, He still intercedes for others through His Spirit dwelling within His people. St. Paul made this point when he wrote, "It makes me happy to suffer for you, as I am suffering now, and in my own body to do what I can to make up all that has still to be undergone by Christ for the sake of his body, the Church." (*Col.* 1:24 TJB).

Suffering in Christ is such a sanctifying experience for oneself and others that it is often the threshold to mystical union with Him. Then we feel the same emotions of sadness, grief, and exhaustion which He felt during His agony. At this time one must be completely receptive to the divine light and respond wholly to the Lord. It is contemplation which helps us in this.

In the strict sense of the word, contemplation is a supernatural love and knowledge of God, simple and obscure, infused by Him into the summit of the soul, giving it a directl contact with Him. Mystical contemplation is an intuition of God born of pure love.[5]

The sufferings and trials that precede the mystical union are so purifying that the Lord, in order to keep a person on this path, often gives him not water from the Rock, but the wine of the Spirit, so that he can endure much. The lovers of God who drink this wine become so intoxicated spiritually that they no longer feel the heavy burden they must bear. The writers of the Old Testament knew of the heavenly wine: "The King has taken me to his banquet hall and the banner he raises over me is love." (*Sg. of Sg.* 2:4 TJB). Here the term "banquet hall" is translated from what literally meant "the house of wine." You will recall that Jesus spoke of His Passion as a cup from which He must drink. (*Jn.* 18:11). And when the disciples were filled with the fire of the Spirit on Pentecost, they were accused of being drunk by observers, who said, "They have been drinking too much new wine." (*Acts* 2:13 TJB). This spiritual wine carries with it the light of knowledge and wisdom; it purifies, heals, and renews. Those who have entered, or will enter, into mystical prayer should ask to be sustained in trials by this sweet wine of martyrs.

Some scholars are of the opinion that a person should not desire the contemplative or mystic way. From my study I have determined that this is wrong thinking. These simple arguments may explain why:

The first case is that of souls that already have a first beginning of mystic graces. It has always been admitted that they may desire to advance in this way, for God has deposited the seed in their souls in order that it may fructify. To desire this is to conform our will to God's will.

The mystic graces are a part of the gifts of the Holy Ghost. Now the church sets us the example of asking for the seven gifts...[6]

Nowadays, if anyone aspires after some gift of prayer a little above the common order he is plainly told . . . that we must not desire them nor ask for them; thus the door of these gifts is forever shut against. This is a great abuse.[7]

In Scripture we often find disciples who have experienced the mystical union with Christ. Some were thus illuminated by the glory of the Divine Presence; others were privileged to share in His sufferings. This was a normal part of the mature Christian life. St. Paul tells us that he experienced the sufferings of Christ in unitive prayer: "I have been crucified with Christ and I live now not with my own life but with the life of Christ who lives in me." (*Gal.* 2:19 TJB). St. Peter also had knowledge of this type of prayer, for he wrote: "If you can have some share in the sufferings of Christ, be glad." (*1 Pt.* 4:13 TJB).

Sooner or later, each Christian will identify with the life of Christ. Some may not be fully aware of this truth, but it is a milestone they must pass as they progress in spiritual life. Jesus calls each one to share in His life in different ways, some of which are hidden. There were many times that I felt this identification with Christ during prayers of infused contemplation or mystical union. At such times I would feel as He must have felt at many times in His life. The following came to me as I experienced the loneliness of the Cross:

The Lanced Word

The word, the lance, 'twas all the same —
It pierced His heart; blood flowed again.
The Savior's blood — 'twas His, now's mine —
His life ebbs away into endless time.
By one sharp word, a death-blow came;
It broke His heart, His love defamed.
Once Heaven's glory, now all forlorn
By denying beasts in human form.
"We knew Him not" — they walked away:
Senseless forms, molded out of clay.

The evil angel had his way, and
Peter cried till the break of day.
It matters not: His friends are gone
Except His holy Mother and John.
Thank You, Father, for such as these;
My painful Passion they helped appease.
Thy wrath, oh, God, Thy Victim's slain;
"We knew Him not," they cried again.
"Father," He cried out to Thee,
"Will You also abandon Me?"
His answer came in painful tones
Of deep silence: "You're all alone.
Complete your work. *Consumatum est!*"
There's an end to endurance;
There is a peace in Thy tomb.

After receiving that word, I realized this truth: Jesus died mainly because He was not received by His own creatures. He was rejected by them and even by those He had chosen, in spite of all He had done to show them His love. The invisible would of unrequited love broke the heart of Christ long before it was pierced by the centurion. Let us look to Scripture to see this truth.

Three times the Lord asked His disciples to stay awake and pray with Him the night before He died. He was practically begging them to comfort Him, for He said to them, "My heart is nearly broken with sorrow." (*Matt.* 26:38 NAB). What a pitiable thought it is that God's beloved Son had to beg ungrateful mankind for their companionship and love. Abandoning Him during His arrest, "all the disciples deserted him and fled." (*Matt.* 26:56 NAB). Judas betrayed Him, Peter denied Him, and the others ran away. The same people who had acclaimed Him as their King on Palm Sunday now sought to murder Him. Though they had seen the signs and wonders that His Father worked through Him, they steeled their hearts against Him and turned away.

Not only the burden of man's sin, but also this rejection was the cause of His death. Even if He had not been tortured and nailed to the Cross to die, He would nevertheless have died of a broken heart. As He hung there upon the Cross, He heard the insults and outrages of the ages as He envisioned the millions who would also turn away. David the Psalmist had been inspired centuries before to see this truth about Jesus' great sorrow when he sang, "Insult has broken my heart ... I looked for sympathy, but there was none; for comforters, and I found none." (*Ps.* 69:21 NAB). And later St. Albert the Great would remark, "For this reason was thy heart wounded, that through the visible wound we might behold the invisible wound of thy love."[8] This invisible wound was that inflicted by the lance of rejection. It broke His heart. "When they came to Jesus ... one of the soldiers pierced his side with a lance; and immediately there came out blood and water." (*Jn.* 19:33, 34 TJB). What could be more defenseless than the exposed, broken heart of the Lamb of God? What more could the Savior have done to prove His love? Meditate seriously upon this and see if you do not find tears in your eyes.

The lamenting voice of the Messiah was silenced; but in that silence a new activity had already begun. Out of that pierced heart flowed the living water of spiritual baptism and the blood of the Eucharist. With the opening of this heart was the release of the gifts of divine grace. Christ is the Pierced One of whom the prophet Zacharias wrote, "They will look on the one whom they have pierced... One that day there shall be opened to the house of David and to the inhabitants of Jerusalem, a fountain to purify from sin and uncleanness." (*Acts* 12:10; 13:1 TJB). It is in this fountain of living waters that the Spirit regenerates the children of God.

In His hour, Jesus found Himself alone. "I called for help to my lovers; they failed me." (*Lam.* 1:19 TJB). How are we failing Him today? By the fact that we refuse to die to our selfishness and sin. We complain in our suffering, seek the easy way out, and convince ourselves that this is good enough. Like the bad thief, we rebel against our destinies. Thus we fall into sin. Christ wants to live in us, but He cannot if our attention is elsewhere. St. Paul teaches, "If we have died with him, then we shall live with him." (*2 Tm.* 2:11 TJB). If we die to sin, the Lord will come to abide with us, even today.

The more closely one is united to Christ here and now, the more he will share in the sufferings of the Savior. This is especially true when one enters into infused contemplation. This form of ecstatic prayer is not easy to explain, but perhaps you will more easily understand it through this experience of mine.

One night, while meditating as I lay down to sleep, I suddenly saw Jesus and Mary in an intellectual vision. The vision lasted throughout the night, on until the next morning. I believe that it was more of the mystic union than anything else, for most visions do not last for a long period of time. I was unable to do anything but receive that which the Lord desired to bestow therein. Fr. Balthazar Alvarez, the spiritual director of St. Theresa of Avila, teaches that their is nothing to fear when one experiences mystical union. Since the experience is wholly spiritual, there is no way for Satan to influence its course.

> If God... "takes from a soul the faculty of reasoning in prayer, it is a sign that He wishes to be in a special way her Master" ...Now none but God alone can penetrate into the interior of the soul, when the doors are closed. Neither the good nor the bad angels have this power; this sign is therefore very certain and *free from illusion*.[9]

St. Theresa of Avila expounds upon the great feeling of jubilation that fills the heart at such times.

> On the "excessive jubilation" felt at times by ecstatics: "May His Majesty often grant us this kind of prayer, which is safe from all danger and most beneficial; we cannot acquire it for ourselves, as it is quite supernatural."[10]

In my own experience of this prayer of union, I felt the loving support of Jesus and Mary, even though it was a prayer of such intense suffering I thought I would die. My body felt bruised and beaten; spiritually I saw and felt welts and blood clots form. Simultaneously, I experienced an anointing of the Holy Spirit, which seemed to flow like a raging fire through my being. "He has sent a fire from on high down into my bones." (*Lam.* 1:13 TJB). This terrible suffering and excessive jubilation alternated and intermingled in such a way that I knew not which was greater. Throughout this unitive prayer, I experienced Mary on the right of me and Jesus on the left side of me, in a supporting way. I did not sleep the entire night, but continually called out the names of Jesus and Mary. Words are not adequate to describe this union further. The only thing I can say is that just as one can experience mystical union with Mary, so too can one experience mystical union with Jesus.

I was unable to find many precedents for this type of intellectual vision. However, St. Jerome, in his letter to Eustochium, describes a similar experience where in a dream he was ordered to be scourged. The only real difference between my experience and his was that he was asleep, whereas I remained awake throughout the night. St. Jerome wrote about his experience of this nature explaining it thus:

> I call to witness the tribunal before which I lay, and the terrible judgment which I feared ... I profess that my shoulders were black and blue, that I felt bruises long after I awoke from my sleep, and that thenceforth, I read the books of God with a zeal greater than I had previously given to the books of men.[11]

How does one explain such deep things of God? The only book I can recommend to the reader to help him to understand this prayer of union would be *The Living Flame of Love*, by St. John of the Cross. He there explains unitive prayer, purifications of the spirit, and other spiritual encounters. He also describes the anointing of the Holy Spirit as a flame of fire:

> Oh, living flame of love
> That tenderly woundest my soul in its deepest center...
> Oh, sweet burn! Oh, delectable wound!...
> That savours of eternal life and pays every debt!
> In slaying, thou hast changed death into life.[12]

Do not fear the crosses and sufferings which come your way, for they will one day become your crowning glory, provided that you accept them in the spirit of the suffering Christ. Embrace them, esteem them as a gift from God, for in truth, they truly are such. It is through our crosses of suffering that we are purged of impurities, that God is glorified, and that our brothers and sisters in Christ are benefitted. I am referring here especially to the types of suffering that come our way for the sake of being Christians. We can do no better than to follow in the footsteps of the Master, who went before us. Throughout your life, you will encounter the Cross under many guises, but the pain can be meritorious if it is offered in union with Christ to the Father. This was the example given to us by the disciples and the saints; we have only to imitate their example to reap an eternal reward.

The sufferings of this world are nothing compared to the glories to come. That time of glory is coming soon when "He will wipe away all tears from their eyes; there will be no more death, and no more mourning or sadness... 'Write this: that what I am saying is sure and will come true.' And then he said, 'It is already done.'" (*Rev.* 21:4-6 TJB).

The Sword of the Spirit

–9–

The Living Stone

Many times God speaks to His people using the language of symbols, for our weak intelligence cannot immediately grasp His revelations. The scholar Poulain explains that

> In visions of Paradise ... God only shows in part
> that reality which is so far beyond our powers of
> understanding. He adapts Himself to our nature
> by making use of symbols.[1]

Looking for and acquiring a sense of Christian symbols will help one gain tremendous powers to interpret and understand the symbolic language of the Bible.

There were times in life when I experienced God speaking to me through symbolism, but I did not understand the meaning of this spiritual language until much later. I will attempt here to illustrate this type of symbolic communication from my own experiences in light of the Scripture.

Once, during prayer time, I became reflective and was thinking about a religious person whom I esteemed very highly, when slowly my mind came to focus upon the holiness of Christ. Then I was given an interior vision wherein the Lord revealed Himself to me symbolically as a Diamond. Simultaneously my understanding was opened to this symbolic image of Christ as the Cornerstone, the Rock, the Living Stone upon which the Messianic Jerusalem would be built.

As I gazed with the spiritual sight upon the huge Diamond, I understood that I was to study this Rock. I reached out to touch this Diamond, and an intense beam of golden light streamed down from above into the center of the Stone. This light was not ordinary light insofar as it was animated with properties which were life-giving. For several minutes this living energy shone down into the Stone and was absorbed by it. I marveled at all that was happening. Slowly I turned the Stone from left to right to examine it from different angles. The golden radiance burned brilliantly within the glittering heart of the Diamond. I realized that this was the Light of God's Glory radiating from its source through numerous facets, magnifying itself, giving new life, virtue, and glory to whomever it came in contact with. I wholeheartedly desired to grasp the total meaning of this vision, and I pondered upon the words which the Spirit of the Lord had also given to me. The following verse accompanied the vision.

A Living Stone

I know that I shall never meet another you,
God's unique one; in all you say and do,
Gladly do I accept each little gift you bring —
A smile, a prayer, the song you sing
As you ripple with laughter, echoing joy,
Feigning nothing,
Alive in Him with His strength of silent peace,
Walking assured in His light,
Becoming ... becoming ... renewed in His life

See there, Oh! the glory of His Being!
Oh, my heart stood still; for
In thee ... I see ... Him,
And in Him I see thee
Reflecting ... reflecting ... reflection
No human eye can see,
A brilliant Diamond, a living stone,
Upon which the light of Yahweh shone.

Then a golden beam in a steady stream of
Living light poured into the heart of you.
Motionless, you absorbed that golden ray
In adoration before His royal throne.
"Come close, my son, and see that
I shall never cease to be.
Come close, come close to Me.
Touch My stone, feel My light.
Gently move Me to the left, to the right."
Then sunburst of living rays of gold.
Each ray had a mystery to unfold
Reflecting Love; the fire glowing within
Reflecting His knowledge like a sage of old;
Reflecting compassion to the lost of the fold.
A thousand reflections and rays were there,
Oh, too much for any human to bear.
My eyes filled with tears at this glorious sight.

Oh Lord! I bow low, oh so low, so low...

Later on I prayed to the Lord to confirm this vision and to teach me more about it. Within a day, my son, unaware of what had happened, came into the house with a small gift. It was a diamond-like crystal with a cross clearly inscribed on top of it. It was a miniature of the Living Stone. I continued to pray for more confirmations; and opening Scripture, I received more teaching concerning this vision.

Further proof of the vision was given to me about a year later during a prayer time when I came across this Scripture in the Bible. It describes the presence of the Lord as He came from a place called Teman as quoted from *Habbakuk* 3:4 (NAB) ... "His splendor spreads like the light, rays shine forth from beside him, where his power is concealed." This was what I had seen in the vision of the Living Stone.

How are we to understand these revelations? "These are the very things," we are told, "that God has revealed to us through the Spirit, for the Spirit reaches the depths of everything, even the depths of God." (*1 Cor.* 2:10 TJB).

Those who have received the outpouring of the Spirit, or the release of the Holy Spirit, will comprehend these things, for "A spiritual man ... is able to judge the value of everything. And his own value is not to be judged by other men." (*1 Cor.* 2:15 TJB).

By being receptive to the Spirit and through the confirmations He gave me, I came to realize that this vision of the Living Stone brought together all of the fragmentary experiences and many blessings He had given me over the years in which I had wandered through the spiritual desert. Now I find myself standing in the Light of His Day and seeing clearly the destination He had set for all Christians from the beginning, the Promised Land of the New Jerusalem. I see His people being empowered with the spiritual gifts of the Holy Spirit so that they may prepare the way for this New Jerusalem and for the Second Coming of the Lord Jesus Christ.

When St. Luke described the first Palm Sunday, he wrote that the people loudly proclaimed the praises of Jesus Christ and reported that, "Some Pharisees in the crowd said to him, 'Master, check your disciples,' but He answered, 'I tell you, if these keep silence, the stones will cry out my praises.'" (*Lk.* 19:39, 40 TJB). In the Twentieth Century, these Stones are calling forth that Kingdom through the prayer of the Holy Spirit. These living gems are the very essence of that spiritual kingdom upon earth and the Light resides within them. And with a committed heart and voice, these people of God cry out, "Marantha!" "Come Lord Jesus, come!"

The magnificent Rock which I saw was faceted into millions of angles in order to reflect more perfectly the numerous attributes, glory, gifts and power of God's Spirit. The Father's precious Stone (Jesus) is not only the Cornerstone of the New Jerusalem, but the perfect pattern from which all the other gems of Jerusalem would be fashioned. God's people are called to reflect not only the image of the Rock, but also the identity and purpose of the Cornerstone as the Lord places them within His foundation.

We know that a diamond is formed under great pressure beneath the earth's surface. That it is buried and hidden very deep is symbolic of humility. We know that a diamond is the strongest, most enduring, and most valuable gem that exists. Nothing can break or cut a diamond except another diamond. In like manner, we are shown that the Master Craftsman chooses His living stones because of their humility, endurance, and strength. These are the stones that readily yield to the carving tool of trials, temptations, and persecutions in order to become the permanent foundation stones for His great spiritual edifice. The Master Craftsman is even now cutting, polishing, and laying these living stones side by side and cementing them together with love, which is the fundamental cohesive element in the Eternal City.

The Scripture passages given to me in prayer also confirmed the vision and were valuable in understanding its interpretation. "In the spirit," Scripture says, "he took me up to the top of an enormous high mountain, and showed me Jerusalem, the holy city, coming down from God out of heaven. It had all the radiant glory of God and glittered like some precious jewel of crystal-clear diamond." (*Rev.* 21:10 TJB).

And also, "It will never be night again and they will not need lamplight or sunlight, because the Lord God will be shining on them. They will reign forever and ever. The angel said to me, 'All that you have written is sure and will come true; the Lord God who gives the spirit to the prophets has sent his angel to reveal to his servants what is soon to take place. Very soon now, I shall be with you again.'" (*Rev.* 22:5-7).

About a week later during prayer, the Lord brought me to still other pertinent verses. One of these was, "Come up here: I will show you what is to come in the future." With that the Spirit possessed me and I saw a throne standing in Heaven, and the One sitting on the throne; and the Person sitting there looked like a diamond." (*Rev.* 4:1-3 TJB). It was this passage which identified for me Who and What the symbolic diamond of this vision was. Oh, I trembled! This was almost identical to what St. John had seen in the Apocalyptic text.

Next I was led to another verse which describes the new priesthood: "Come to him a living stone, rejected by men but approved nonetheless, and precious in God's eyes. You too are living stones, built as an edifice of spirit, into a holy priesthood, offering spiritual sacrifices, acceptable to God through Jesus Christ. For Scripture has it: 'See, I am laying a cornerstone in Zion, an approved stone, and precious. He who puts his faith in it shall not be shaken.'" (*1 Pt.* 2:6 NAB). I now saw that in this vision the Lord had been present to me as the living Cornerstone filled with the Shakinah Light of glory and that He was promising to bring forth through the power of His Spirit other living stones as His priests, for "you ... are a chosen race, a royal priesthood, a consecrated nation, a people set apart to sing the praises of God who called you out of darkness into his wonderful light. Once you were no people, but now you are God's people." (*1 Pt.* 2:9 TJB).

The Lord has called those who believe in Him to be a "kingdom of priests and kings to serve our God, and they shall reign on the earth." (*Rev.* 5:10 TJB). This holy nation, born of God, is even now offering up to the Father praise in the Spirit. "Indeed it is just such worshippers that the Father seeks." (*Jn.* 4:23 NAB). This spiritual priesthood, anointed by the Holy Spirit, was appointed to give glory to His name. "Through him let us continually offer God the sacrifice of praise, that is the fruit of lips which acknowledge his name." (*Heb.* 13:15 NAB).

In the Old Testament, we see that King Solomon appointed thousands of men to sing God's praises before he began constructing the fabulous Temple. This foreshadowed what is happening in the world. Especially within the last fifteen years there has been a tremendous outpouring of the charismatic gift of praise, and this perfected praise will precede the erection of the Messianic Jerusalem, where God will dwell with His covenant people. Although this magnificent work has already begun, it is not readily apparent to most people as it can only be perceived in a spiritual way.

The Lord enabled me to arrive at an understanding of these things through the means of ecstatic prayer. He brought me, in the spirit, to the heavenly Jerusalem when I was but a child of seven years old. This glimpse of Heaven took place in an ecstatic rapture which the Lord bestowed immediately following the reception of sacramental communion. This might seem highly improbable, but you will recall the many examples of children who were cited in Chapter 1 who also experienced this state of rapture. This is part of the mystic union which may or may not take place during the reception of the Sacraments. When this rapture took place, within a single moment the Spirit of God transported me to a great height and distance, and from that height showed me the Heavenly Jerusalem which was to come. With wondering eyes, I looked down upon a fabulous transparent city which seemed to glow and glitter with radiance of His divine Light, making it intensely bright and luminous. Everything that I perceived within this City was pulsating with this living Light. All the buildings, walls, and streets were transparent and crystal-clear because of this radiating Light. There was a very high wall surrounding this celestial City, and the Spirit brought me down from a great height to a gateway within the wall. On either side of this opening stood two enormously tall angels. I stood there on the threshold and looked upon a truly glorious sight. Then suddenly, everything vanished and I was still kneeling in the church trying in some childish way to say, "Thank you, Jesus," but I was speechless and lost for words.

This spiritual perception of Jerusalem moved me to run home to the privacy of my room, and I tried to somehow recapture that scene by drawing it on paper. I hid this childish masterpiece from sight and kept that moment treasured in my heart. The depth of this mystery was so enormous that I could not grasp it totally and kept it buried silently in my spirit. For some unknown reason, I never told anyone about it. It was not until the vision of the Living Stone took place that fragments of a lifetime began to piece together.

As the years progressed, I learned that "In a deep ecstasy, God unites the soul suddenly to His Essence, and when He fills her with His light, He shows her in a moment of time, the sublimest mysteries and all His secret things."[2] For forty years, the Lord was teaching me, as it were, to appreciate more fully that which He had given throughout my lifetime. When the Lord granted me the vision of the Living Stone, I suddenly saw the events of grace coming together to form a complete picture of what is happening in our age; that is, the birth of God's Kingdom, here and now. Oh, it is so spiritual, so hidden; yet, it is evolving before our very eyes.

St. John the Evangelist tells us what to do until that glorious day comes in perfect fulfillment. He said, "While you have the light, keep faith in the light; thus you will become sons of light." (*Jn.* 12:36 NAB). The more closely we identify ourselves with Christ through His Spirit, the greater will be our capacity to receive from Him this Living Light and to transmit it, like His living Stone, into the world. Jesus will make you sons of light when you have cleansed your hearts of all stains of sin. Bathe yourselves in the Blood of the

Lamb! Wash yourselves clean so that He may fill you with the Light of His Life, making you a lamp of glory capable of transforming the darkness around your milieu.

Sing praise to the Lamb, to the Lord your God, all you His people! Raise your voice in anticipation and joy. Cry out to Him, "Come Lord Jesus!" Enter these celestial gates with great thanksgiving, for the Holy One will place His seal upon you as the day of Redemption draws near. "The Spirit and the Bride say, 'Come. Let everyone who listens answer, Come. Then let all who are thirsty come; all who want it may have the water of life, and have it free.'" (*Rev.* 22:17 TJB). And the living stones will echo, "Come, Lord Jesus! Maranatha!

Notes

Many Scripture texts used in this book are taken from *The New American Bible* (NAB), copyright 1970, by the Confraternity of Christian Doctrine, Washington, D.C., and are used by permission of the copyright owner. All rights reserved.

Other Scripture excerpts are from *The Jerusalem Bible* (TJB), copyright 1966, by Darton, Longman, and Todd, Ltd., and Doubleday and Company, Inc., and are used by permission of the publisher.

CHAPTER 1

[1] Dom Vitalis Lehody, *Ways of Mental Prayer,* trans. a monk of Mount Mellery (Dublin: M.H. Gill and Son, 1960), p. 399.
[2] Dr. Imbert-Goubeyre, *La stigmatisation et l'extase divine,* cited in *The Graces of Interior Prayer*, by A. Poulain, trans. Leonora L. Yorke Smith (St. Louis: Herder, 1950), pp. 245-246.

CHAPTER 2

[1] Life, cited by Poulain, ibid., p. 240.
[2] Ibid., pp. 299-300.

CHAPTER 3

[1] Poulain, *op. cit.*, pp. 349-350.
[2] Adolphe Tanquerey, *The Spiritual Life: A Treatise on Ascetical and Mystical Theology,* trans. Herman Branderis (Tournai: Desclee, 1930), p. 633.

CHAPTER 4

1. *True Devotion to Mary,* trans. Frederick W. Faber (Bay Shore, NY: Montfort, 1956), p. 28.
2. Cited by John Ferrarro, *Ten Series of Meditations on the Mysteries of the Rosary* (Boston: Daughters of St. Paul, 1964), p. 65.
3. Gabriel Denis, *The Reign of Jesus Through Mary* (Bay Shore: Montfort, 1949), p. 25.
4. Ibid., p. 11.
5. Cited in Ferrarro, *op. cit.*, p. 220.
6. *Vie Mariale de maria a Sancta Teresia,* cited in *Anthology of Mysticism*, ed. Paul de Jaegher, trans. Donald A. Attwater et. al., (Westminster, MD: Newman Press, 1950), pp. 208-211.
7. George Maloney, *The Mystic of Fire and Light: St. Symeon, the New Theologian* (Denville, NJ: Dimension, 1975), pp. 107-108.
8. *Immaculata Review,* #B 1-1, Tab 2 Sect. 22 (September, 1976), p. 1.
9. The Revelations, cited by Sr. Mary Jeremy, *Scholars and Mystics* (Chicago, Henry Regnery, 1962), pp. 261-262.
10. *True Devotion to Mary, op. cit.*, pp. 38-40.
11. Cited by Ferrarro, *op. cit.*, p. 229.

CHAPTER 5

1. Morton T. Kelsey, *Dreams: The Dark Speech of the Spirit, a Christian Interpretation* (Garden City, NY: Doubleday, 1968), p. 153.
2. *Commentary on Acts,* cited ibid., p. 140.
3. Laurent Volken, *Visions, Revelations and the Church,* trans. Edward Gallagher (New York: P.J. Kennedy, 1963), p. 160.
4. Augustine Fitzpatrick, *Essays and Hymns of Synesius of Cyrene*, cited in Kelsey, *op. cit.*, p. 143.
5. Poulain, *op. cit.*, pp. 301-302.
6. Benedict Pererius de Magia, *Concerning the Investigation of Dreams and Concerning Astrological Divinations. Three Books Against the False and Superstitious Art* (sic.), cited by Kelsey, *op. cit.,* p. 292.
7. Letter LI, 14 cited by Kelsey, ibid., p. 145.
8. Kelsey, ibid., p. 37.

9 Ibid., pp. 146-147.

10 Ibid., p. 36.

11 *Vie,* cited by Poulain, *op. cit.,* p. 268.

12 Denis, *op. cit.,* p. 120.

13 Kelsey, *op. cit.,* p. 153.

14 Benedict Pererius de Magia, *op. cit.,* p. 306.

15 Kelsey, *op. cit.,* pp. 153-154.

16 Poulain, *op. cit.,* p. 292.

17 *Homo Apostolicus,* cited by Poulain, ibid., p. 266.

18 Poulain, ibid., pp. 264-265.

19 Volken, *op. cit.,* pp. 244-245.

20 St. Theresa of Avila, *Interior Castle,* cited by Poulain, *op. cit.,* p. 241.

21 Poulain, ibid., p. 244.

22 Ibid., p. 254.

23 Ibid., p. 245.

24 *Lucerna mystica,* cited by Poulain, ibid., p. 354.

25 Poulain, ibid., p. 252.

26 Ibid., p. 395.

27 Ibid., p. 381.

28 St. Bonaventure, *De septum itineribus aeternitatis,* cited by Poulain, *op. cit.,* p. 101.

29 *Interior Castle,* ibid., p. 267.

30 Poulain, ibid., p. 249.

31 *Interior Castle,* ibid., pp. 266-267. Italics by Poulain.

32 Pierre Teilhard De Chardin, *Hymn of the Universe* (New York: Harper Colophon, 1969), pp. 68-69.

33 Ibid., p. 71.

34 Venerable Blosius, *A Book of Spiritual Instruction,* cited by Poulain, *op. cit.,* p. 473.

35 Poulain, ibid., p. 474.

CHAPTER 6

1 *Sermons and Conferences,* cited by H.A. Reinhold, ed., *The Soul Afire, Revelations of the Mystics* (Garden City: Image, 1973), p. 374.

2   St. Ambrose, cited in *With Bright Wings, A Book of the Spirit,* ed. Mary Grace Swift (New York: Paulist, 1976), p. 103.

3   Felix Timmermans, *The Perfect Joy of St. Francis,* trans. Raphael Brown (Garden City: Image, 1955), p. 79.

4   Fioretti, "St. Francis of Assisi and Christ" in Reinhold, *op. cit.,* p. 266.

5   Marie Tessonier, cited by Reinhold, ibid., p. 365.

6   Maloney, *op. cit.,* p. 188.

7   St. Alphonsus Rodriguez, *Vie,* cited by Poulain, *op. cit.,* p. 228.

8   Alvarez de Paz, *De Inquisitone pacis sive de studio oratione,* cited by Poulain, ibid., p. 282.

9   Ibid., p. 76.

10   Johannes Steiner, *The Visions of Therese Neumann* (New York: Alba House, 1976), p. 56.

11   Ibid., p. 58.

12   Timmermans, *op. cit.,* p. 109.

13   Anne Catherine Emmerich, *The Life of the Blessed Virgin Mary,* trans. Sir Michael Palairet (Springfield, IL: Templegate, 1954), pp. 192-193.

14   *Commentary on the Song of Songs*, cited by George A. Maloney, *The Breath of the Mystic* (Denville, NJ: Dimension, 1974), p. 75.

15   Cited by Reinhold, *op. cit.,* p. 277.

16   St. John of the Cross, *Dark Night of the Soul,* trans. E. Allison Peers (Garden City: Image, 1962), pp. 117-118.

17   Reinhold, *op. cit.,* p. 368.

18   Ibid., p. 48.

19   "First Sermon for the Second Sunday after the Epiphany," cited by Poulain, *op. cit.,* p. 272.

CHAPTER 7

1   Francis MacNutt, *Healing,* Notre Dame: Ave Maria Press, 1974, p. 3

2   Michael Harper, *Spiritual Warfare* (Plainfield, NJ: Logos, 1970), pp. 61-62.

CHAPTER 8

1. *Love of Eternal Wisdom,* trans. A. Sommers (Bay Shore: Montfort, 1960), pp. 88, 93, 97-98.
2. *Interior Castles,* trans. E. Allison Peers (Garden City: Image, 1961), p. 227.
3. *Love of Eternal Wisdom,* op. cit., p. 94.
4. Reinhold, *op. cit.,* p. 336.
5. Thomas Merton, *What is Contemplation?* (London: Burns, Oates & Washbourne, 1956), p. 11.
6. Poulain, *op. cit.,* pp. 458-459.
7. Louis Lallement, *La Doctrine Spirituelle,* cited by Poulain, *op. cit.,* p. 476.
8. Cited in *Heart of the Savior,* by Josef Stierli, et. al., ed., trans. Paul Andrews (St. Louis: Herder, 1967), p. 78.
9. *Le Guide Spirituel,* cited by Poulain, *op. cit.,* p. 476.
10. Poulain, ibid., p. 463.
11. Cited by Kelsey, *op. cit.,* p. 152.
12. St. John of the Cross, "Stanzas Made by the Soul in the Intimate Union of God," trans. E. Allison Peers (Garden City: Image, 1962), p. 152.

CHAPTER 9

1. Poulain, *op. cit.,* p. 329.
2. Ibid., p. 275.